Marking Native Borders

Marking Native Borders

Indigenous Geography and American Empire in the Early Tennessee Country

LUCAS P. KELLEY

UNIVERSITY OF OKLAHOMA PRESS : NORMAN

Library of Congress Cataloging-in-Publication Data

Names: Kelley, Lucas P., author.
Title: Marking native borders : indigenous geography and American empire in the
    early Tennessee country / Lucas Kelley.
Description: Norman : University of Oklahoma Press, [2025] | Includes bibliograph-
    ical references and index. | Summary: "Details how, in the late colonial and early
    republic periods, the Cherokees and Chickasaws defended their permanent, inherent
    right to their lands in the Tennessee Country (the region drained by the Tennessee,
    Cumberland, and Mississippi rivers and their tributaries) by drawing clear borders
    around their nations and combining Indigenous ideas of communal land use with
    aspects of European property law. The book also describes how white settlers and
    speculators, in turn, revised their own strategies for expansion in response to the
    Cherokees' and Chickasaws' success in defending their national lands"—Provided
    by publisher.
Identifiers: LCCN 2024042373 | ISBN 9780806195414 (hardcover)
Subjects: LCSH: Cherokee Indians—Land tenure—Tennessee River Region—History—
    18th century. | Chickasaw Indians—Land tenure—Tennessee River Region—
    History—18th century.
Classification: LCC E99.C5 K387 2025 | DDC 976.8/0200497—dc23/eng/20250203
LC record available at https://lccn.loc.gov/2024042373

The paper in this book meets the guidelines for permanence and durability of the
Committee on Production Guidelines for Book Longevity of the Council on Library
Resources, Inc. ∞

For Emma

Contents

Acknowledgments

It seems to be customary for most acknowledgments to start by identifying professional colleagues, sources of research funding, academic mentors, or other information related to a book's publication. Although all of these details appear below, I can begin no other way than by mentioning my wife, Emma Kelley. The love and support that she has shown me throughout this project has been unwavering. She truly is exceptional in so many ways. It is to Emma that I dedicate this book.

I owe a profound debt of gratitude to all of the people who have contributed to my understanding and interpretation of the history that appears in these pages. Harry Watson has had the greatest impact on me as a scholar and provided insightful guidance on all stages of this project. Kathleen DuVal offered enthusiastic suggestions and thoughtful critiques of my interpretations of early American history and borderlands methodologies. I doubt I would have ever appreciated the historical significance of Native peoples had I not had the opportunity to learn from Malinda Lowery. Our canoe trip down the Lumbee River showed me the contemporary importance of this history. William Barney made this project better by asking hard questions at the right times. Laura Edwards influenced my understanding of legal history, but I will forever appreciate that she always made time to provide feedback on numerous chapter drafts as an external member of my dissertation committee. This book benefitted tremendously from numerous conversations and input in both formal and informal settings. Maggie Blackhawk, Rebecca Goetz, Rachel Herrmann, Angela Pulley Hudson, Ebony Jones, Patty Limerick, Warren Milteer, Jamie Myers, David Nichols, Julie Reed, Keith Richotte, Jessica Roney, Honor Sachs, Samantha Seeley, Silvana Siddali, Rose Stremlau, Robinson Woodward-Burns, and the late Jenny Tone-Pah-Hote all provided feedback on chapters, conference papers, and workshop presentations. Andrew Frank, Jason Herbert, Aubrey

Lauersdorf, Jamie Myers, Evan Nooe, Greg O'Brien, Julie Reed, and Jeff Washburn have enriched my understanding of the Native South. Patricia Dawson encouraged me to think more about Cherokee language and material culture, and Garrett Wright shared his understanding of the Native history field in my early years as a graduate student. Eric Beccera, Robert Colby, Isaiah Ellis, Caroline Newhall, and Emma Rothberg read the earliest iterations of this book, and its final version is better because of their brilliance. Gabe Moss helped me recognize the geographical and spatial aspects of the Tennessee Country. I must thank Tom Seabrook for editing early drafts of this entire manuscript. Jesse Curtis, Chuck Schaefer, and Colleen Seguin have been excellent colleagues in Valparaiso University's history department, and I thank them for their advice and encouragement in this book's final stages. Finally, I need to thank my anonymous reviewers, my editor Alessandra Tamulevich, and the other editorial staff at the University of Oklahoma Press for seeing this project's potential and guiding it through the publication process.

Various institutions and organizations provided support for this book. The Tennessee Historical Society, the Graduate School at the University of North Carolina, UNC's history department, the Center for the Study of the American South, the North Caroliniana Society, and Valparaiso University contributed important funding for research, travel, and publication. The Royster Society of Fellows at UNC allowed me to take a year off from my graduate school teaching obligations at a crucial stage of this project. I wish to thank archivists and staff at the Filson Historical Society, the William L. Clements Library at the University of Michigan, Harvard University's Houghton Library, the Massachusetts Historical Society, the South Caroliniana Library at the University of South Carolina, the Rubenstein Rare Book and Manuscript Library at Duke University, the Alabama Department of Archives and History, the Georgia Archives, the Library of Congress, the National Archives, the Library of Virginia, the Historical Society of Pennsylvania, Tulane University Special Collections, the Betsey B. Creekmore Special Collections and University Archives at the University of Tennessee at Knoxville, the Chattanooga Public Library, the Calvin M. McClung Historical Collection of the Knox County Public Library, the Knox County Archives, Hunter Library Special Collections at Western Carolina University, and the Tennessee State Library and Archives. Staff at the Rauner Special Collections Library at Dartmouth University digitized an entire collection for me. The American Philosophical Society deserves special thanks not only for allowing me to conduct research in its fantastic collections but also for hosting an academic conference that provided invaluable feedback and professional connections. Portions of this book were previously published by the American Philosophical Society as "Clear Boundaries or Shared Territory: Chickasaw and Cherokee Resistance to American Colonization, 1785–1816," *Transactions of the American Philosophical Society* 110, part 4 (2021): 93–116. I became a regular fixture for several years at the State Archives of North Carolina, and I wish to thank personally Doug Brown, Erin Fulp, and Josh Hagar, who helped identify relevant records and collections. Biff Hollingsworth, Chaitra Powell, Jason Tomberlin, and Matt Turi all influenced this project through their incredible knowledge of resources housed in the Southern Historical Collection and the Wilson Library. They made the University of North Carolina at Chapel Hill an amazing place to study Native history and southern history. The interlibrary loan staff at Valparaiso University's Christopher Center Library procured essential materials during the final stages of this book.

Friends and family members constantly encouraged my academic pursuits long before I read the first primary source that appears in these pages. Alex Hurley, Will Nisbet, Ryan Pierce, and Andy Vinson deserve thanks for providing me with necessary breaks from the researching and writing process. Parker Lawson, a scholar in his own right, has read portions of this project and has been a confidant regarding all aspects of graduate school and the academic job market. My friend and former teammate Brenton Deal was kind enough to allow me to stay with him for several weeks while researching in Nashville. Paul Quigley taught me how to be a historian while I was a graduate student at Virginia Tech. I thank him for his continued advice and friendship over the years. During my time in graduate school, the Norris family made North Carolina feel like home. Anne and Bill Norris remain the most generous and loving in-laws I could ever ask for, and Anne Elizabeth and TJ Bugbee are the sister and brother I've never had. This project is older than my nephew Brooks, but he has already added so much joy to my life. Beth Norris has made me feel like one of her own grandchildren. I thank her especially for opening her home to me during several research trips to Raleigh and Chapel Hill. Despite living on the other side of the country, my uncle, John Kelley, always makes time to celebrate my achievements and successes. My grandparents Norma and Paul Kelley did not live to see this project's conclusion, but their influence on me remains. I am a historian because of my grandfather. Whether it was driving around Knoxville's historic sites, ambling through McMinn County cow pastures searching for family cemeteries, or visiting Fort Loudoun, he made me appreciate the past's impact on the present.

My grandmother believed that education makes the world a better place. I only hope that I can have such a positive impact in my career as she did in her forty years teaching public school students in North Knoxville. My grandparents Eugene and Barbara McCammon continue to shape my life. Maybe one day I will be as well-read as my grandfather, though I doubt I will ever have as many books. My grandmother was my first teacher. I'll never forget learning to read and write as I sat beside her at the dining room table. My parents, Melinda and Michael Kelley, always have been my greatest cheerleaders. They taught me the value of hard work and instilled in me an appreciation for learning. I'm fortunate to be their son.

Introduction

Marking Boundaries on the Map

In late summer 1792, Piominko (Mountain Leader), Wolf's Friend (Ugulaya-cabe), and other Chickasaw leaders traveled to Nashville, a tiny American out-post on the banks of the Cumberland River. They did so at the behest of William Blount, governor of the Southwest Territory. Blount, serving in his current role since the creation of the federally administered territory nearly three years earlier, desperately wanted to formalize the existing peace between the United States and the Chickasaw Nation and the Choctaw Nation, whose representatives had accompanied the Chickasaw diplomats on their journey to Nashville. U.S. president George Washington and his secretary of war, Henry Knox, were in the midst of a developing crisis north of the Ohio River where, a year earlier, a powerful confederacy of Native nations had destroyed Arthur St. Clair's army of federal troops. With the Native confederacy's expanding power to the north, Creek and Cherokee opposition to white settlements in Georgia and the South-west Territory, and Spain's growing influence in the Mississippi Valley, the United States needed the Chickasaws and Choctaws to remain its allies.[1]

Chickasaws, however, had their own plans for the Nashville conference. Their goal was to convince representatives of the United States to accept the existing boundaries of the Chickasaw Nation and acknowledge Chickasaws' undisputed sovereignty within this territory, a concession they had secured from Spain only two months before. On the second day of the conference, Piominko declared his "wish to have the boundaries settled" and outlined his interpretation of the Chickasaw Nation's geographical limits based on the Treaty of Hopewell, nego-tiated with the United States in 1786. His message was a pointed critique of a more recent U.S. treaty with the Cherokee Nation in which he understood "the Cherokees claimed all Duck river" land in their negotiations with the federal government.[2] Piominko wanted the American commissioners to realize that

1

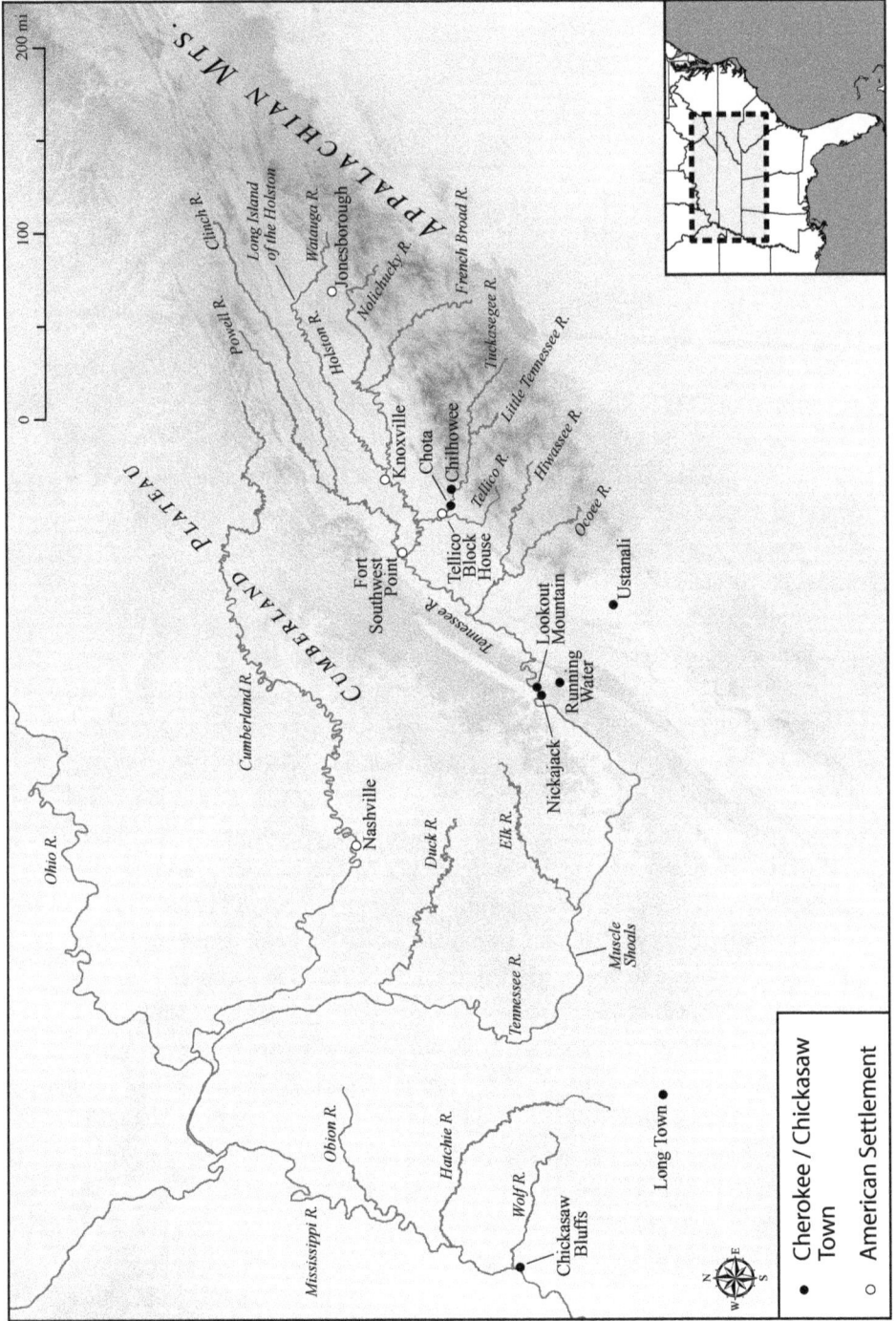

The Tennessee Country. Map created by Gabe Moss on behalf of the author.

Cherokee / Chickasaw Town

American Settlement

Cherokees could not cede any of the land in question because it belonged to the Chickasaw Nation.

Piominko and the other Chickasaw diplomats faced stiff opposition. It was not the Americans who rejected Chickasaws' proposed borders. Rather, the few Cherokees at the conference challenged Piominko because of his overarching understanding of boundary lines between Native nations. Nontuaka (The Northward), a prominent Cherokee official from Cheestowee Town, acknowledged that Cherokees considered the Duck River watershed to be within their national limits. There was no reason, however, why Chickasaws could not claim the territory for their nation as well. In recent negotiations with U.S. officials, Cherokees had described much of the Tennessee Country—the watery environment of the Tennessee and Cumberland Valleys and the minor waterways flowing west to the Mississippi River in what is now western Kentucky and Tennessee—as "the common hunting ground" of the Cherokees, Chickasaws, Creeks, and Choctaws. It was perfectly acceptable, echoed Nontuaka, for Chickasaws and Cherokees to share territory, but he "never knew, before the present, that our people divided land and made lines like white people."[3] Nontuaka agreed that there should be a clear boundary separating the United States from Native nations but saw no reason for Indigenous peoples to demarcate boundaries among themselves.

Chickasaws countered that clear boundary lines were essential, regardless of whether they divided Native peoples' territory from the United States or Native nations from one another. Piominko had intentionally described the Chickasaw Nation's territorial limits at the Hopewell conference "to save my own land," knowing "the fondness of the Cherokees to sell land." He did not want closed borders, and he welcomed all Indigenous peoples to hunt in the Chickasaw Nation. Yet, with other Native nations making cessions to the federal government, it was more important than ever for all parties to understand the proper limits of Chickasaw sovereignty. Wolf's Friend agreed with Piominko. "It is right to mark our boundaries on the map," he told Nontuaka. Before leaving Nashville, Chickasaws did just that by outlining their national borders for U.S. negotiators.[4]

Piominko, Wolf's Friend, and the other Chickasaws at the Nashville conference were proposing a novel break from existing Indigenous notions of space and territory. Native southerners had long shared the Tennessee Country. The Choctaw diplomat Shot-in-Mouth considered the Nashville conference to be taking place literally "in the middle ground." By demanding a clear border between the Chickasaw Nation and the Cherokee Nation, Piominko and Wolf's Friend envisioned a future where Native nations marked their territorial limits, exerted undisputed sovereignty within them, and maintained property rights over their national lands. White Americans' appetite for Native land would only increase in the coming years. Peaceful diplomacy and clear boundaries offered a potential check on speculators' and settlers' invasion of Chickasaw hunting territory. Cherokees like Nontuaka considered their people's claims to the Tennessee Country to be just as legitimate as those of the Chickasaw Nation and resented Chickasaws' insistence that their nation owned portions of the region outright.[5]

These 1792 negotiations at Nashville reveal how the competing geographies among Chickasaws, Cherokees, and white expansionists shaped the process of American empire and influenced Native sovereignty. From the moment European invaders first trudged over the Appalachian Mountains in the 1770s, Native peoples and white colonists reimagined and recreated the space and territory of the Tennessee Country to both defend their national lands and facilitate ongoing expansion. The constant, often violent and coerced interactions between Chickasaws and Cherokees, Europeans and Americans in the Tennessee Country influenced how the region's stakeholders understood the connection between territory and sovereignty, the authority their nations and states exercised over territory.[6] When white intruders began to encroach on Native land, either as settlers or speculators, Cherokees and Chickasaws fortified their national territory by creating clear borders around their nations. They further defended their permanent, inherent right to these bordered spaces by combining their existing Indigenous conceptions of land use with aspects of European property law, thereby laying claim to their territories in ways that conformed to notions of property rights emerging throughout the Atlantic World. Chickasaws and Cherokees successfully defended their nations' sovereignty and property for decades against Americans' expansionist schemes.

To combat the persistence of Native polities, white Americans themselves devised new geographical understandings in their attempt to construct a settler empire in the Tennessee Country. Many shared the sentiments of "the frontier people of the state of Tennessee." Facing eviction from the Cherokee Nation by federal troops in 1797, these anonymous authors of an editorial in the *Knoxville Gazette* freely admitted to settling "within what is called the indian boundary." They defended their actions by claiming the "divine right" to "cultivate and convert to our use any unappropriated part of the habitable globe."[7] Any check on expansion was illegitimate. Settlers and speculators ultimately acquired Native territory by shaping American law and U.S. governance to suit their expansionist geographies. Confronting the bordered sovereignty of the Chickasaw Nation and the Cherokee Nation, land speculators disconnected property rights from jurisdiction, which allowed them to commodify land within Native borders and invest in future dispossession. Local white inhabitants did not just ignore Cherokee and Chickasaw bounds; they insisted that the only legitimate government was one that secured their property rights to stolen Native land. The story of the Tennessee Country in the late eighteenth and early nineteenth centuries includes a series of locally responsive governments that white intruders controlled from the margins. Theirs was a contested project that culminated with several land cession treaties between the United States and the Chickasaw and Cherokee Nations in the 1810s.

White Americans imagined their own version of empire in the decades after U.S. independence. Although they opposed British imperial rule, inhabitants of the United States did not necessarily oppose empire and the territorial expansion that accompanied it. Many just hoped to appropriate imperialism for their own uses.[8] Scholars, however, disagree about how this imagined empire took shape. In analyses that explore the territory north of the Ohio River, historians emphasize the activity of the federal government, with its administration of public lands and mobilization of U.S. troops. A similar process would later play out along the Gulf Coast and Lower Mississippi Valley, as the Native South became "slave country."[9] Events in the Tennessee Country necessitate an alternate understanding of American empire. By insisting that the only legitimate government was one that facilitated ongoing dispossession, white Americans in the Tennessee Country imagined a "bottom-up, settler-driven" empire that could survive without the aid of federal troops or the reward of public lands. Cherokees and Chickasaws certainly encountered American imperialism in the decades after U.S. independence, but the empire that took shape was much more insidious than the more obvious presence of the federal government in the Old Northwest.[10] Yet despite tired teleological depictions of early America "as proto-nationalist spaces whose stories are the seedbed for modern nation-states" and accompanying projections of colonial empires and contemporary nations onto maps of North America, the U.S. empire that did emerge over the course of the nineteenth century was contested and remains incomplete. Native peoples resisted European colonization, maintained power and sovereignty, and continue to persist against settler erasure.[11]

The proliferation of studies that explore early America from Native peoples' perspective is due, in part, to historians' burgeoning emphasis on North American borderlands. Borderlands historians once focused primarily on the global implications of events in peripheral zones of contact between competing

European empires. These borderlands were sites where the interactions between Indigenous peoples and European newcomers created unique cultures and political economies that differed from developments in the imperial center. Over time, explained Jeremy Adelman and Stephen Aron, "colonial borderlands gave way to national borders," curtailing Native power and destroying the cultural, political, and economic distinctiveness of these previous zones of contact. Despite the attempt of Adelman and Aron to create a useful framework for borderlands scholarship, subsequent historians soon critiqued their interpretations. Many believed that their borderlands-to-bordered-land model exaggerated European empires and subsequent nation-states as the driving force of historical change. Indeed, recent scholarship has revealed how Indigenous peoples maintained their territory, guarded their sovereignty, and preserved their cultures within the bordered landscape of the nation-state.[12]

Scholars are right to question Adelman and Aron's conclusions, but in challenging their declension narrative of Native power as borderlands became bordered land, historians mostly have overlooked the *borders* in these borderlands. Although it is certainly true that white Americans and Native peoples created a unique borderland society in the Tennessee Country, Chickasaws and Cherokees also sought to divide themselves from one another and from white expansionists as a way to protect their lands. Native peoples had always known their nations' boundaries, but surveying their borders provided a means to define the limits of their national sovereignty, even after the United States claimed jurisdiction over all territory east of the Mississippi River.[13] Recovering Indigenous peoples' support for clear boundary lines adds necessary complexity to scholars' borderlands methodologies and their interpretations of Native persistence against U.S. expansion. A bordered landscape did not mark the end of Native power, nor did it destroy the unique cross-cultural interactions among residents of the eighteenth- and early nineteenth-century Tennessee Country.

African Americans, both enslaved and free, experienced the effects of American empire and Native sovereignty in the Tennessee Country as well. The dispossession of Native peoples facilitated the massive geographical expansion of slavery in the nineteenth century. The connection between slavery and dispossession was particularly visible in Tennessee and North Carolina. It should come as no surprise that in the same decade that architects of American empire expelled Cherokees from their Tennessee Country homelands, after concocting new notions regarding people of color's permanent racial inferiority, they also disfranchised free men of color in Tennessee's 1834 constitution and North

Carolina's 1835 constitution. African Americans employed their own imagined geographies of the Tennessee Country. The region's unstable and evolving jurisdictional boundaries offered a potential escape from bondage. Enslaved and free people of color challenged borders' legitimacy by crossing the numerous boundaries of the Tennessee Country, even as growing numbers of Chickasaws and Cherokees embraced the plantation slavery of their white American neighbors.[14] Nevertheless, this book is grounded in the lives of Chickasaws, Cherokees, white settlers, and land speculators, because they possessed the necessary authority to devise, construct, and enforce the numerous boundaries found throughout the Tennessee Country borderlands.

The Tennessee Country, in particular, offers an especially useful setting for analyzing the competing geographies among Native peoples and white expansionists. Although the region may seem marginal in broader conversations about the Atlantic World, "the margins," explain historians Christopher Grasso and Karin Wulf, "can be the very places that define an empire." Events in the Tennessee Country, as in all of the trans-Appalachian West, had widespread implications that reverberated far beyond the watersheds of the Tennessee, Cumberland, and Mississippi Rivers. It was here where an American empire took shape and survived without—and often in spite of—the efforts of U.S. leaders, and it was here where Native persistence threatened the very foundations of this empire.[15] Generations of Chickasaws and Cherokees, as well as other Indigenous peoples, had called the rugged mountains and rich bottomlands of the Tennessee Country home long before Europeans began coveting their land. The watery landscape itself was of great cultural significance for Indigenous peoples. "Tennessee," the name of both the region's most prominent river system and the U.S. state that ultimately exercised jurisdiction over most of its area, is itself derived from "Tenasi," the name of a Cherokee town once located along the Little Tennessee River in the foothills of the Appalachian Mountains. Early European maps of North America identified the Tennessee River as the Cherokee River and labeled a tributary of the Mississippi as the Chickasaw River. People familiar with the region knew of the Chickasaws' historic settlement at the Chickasaw Old Fields in the Tennessee River's Great Bend.[16] Indigeneity defined the Tennessee Country's landscape.

Marking Native Borders explores the competing geographies, conflicting sovereignty claims, and disputed property rights of Native and white inhabitants of the Tennessee Country. It was in the 1760s that Cherokees and Chickasaws first began to favor clear borders to define the limits of their nations' sovereignty. Chapter 1 situates these new international borders within the broader historical

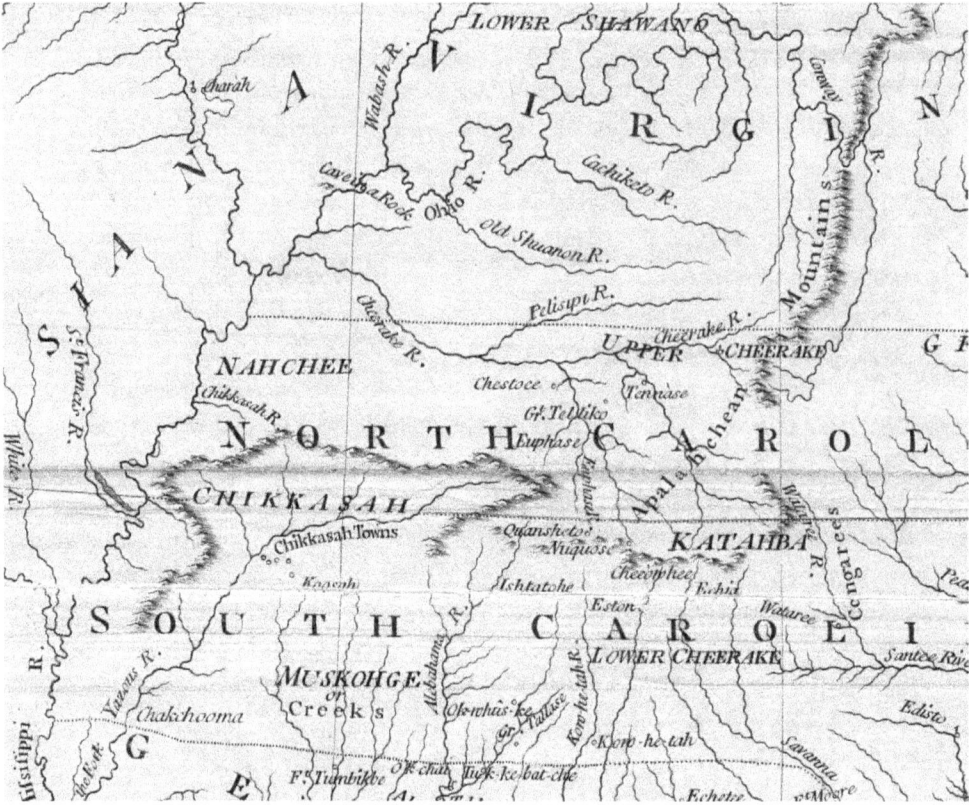

A Map of the American Indian Nations, 1775. North Carolina Maps, University of
North Carolina. This map, drawn by a British mapmaker, depicts the Tennessee Country's
Indigenous landscape. The Tennessee River is named for the Cherokee Nation, and
the map locates the Cherokee town "Tennase" along the Little Tennessee River.
The short "Chikkasah" River flows into the Mississippi.

context of the Atlantic World. Native peoples' manipulation of space disrupted
settler expansion and shaped the relationship between white stakeholders of
the Tennessee Country and distant colonial, state, and national governments.
Chapter 2 traces the multifaceted attempts of eastern speculators, local settlers,
and state governments to secure Cherokee and Chickasaw territory for white
expansion in the wake of U.S. independence. White settlers and speculators took
little notice of Native sovereignty and began to envision an expansive American empire, despite U.S. officials' reluctance to support this imperial project.

Chapter 3 chronicles the failure of U.S. governance, even as the federal government established the Southwest Territory to administer the Tennessee Country directly beginning in 1789. The lack of federal authority further alienated Cherokees, Chickasaws, and white settlers from the United States and incentivized their ongoing attempts to either secure their national territory or construct a government that could enact their local visions for further expansion. As the region's white residents organized the state of Tennessee in 1796, Native leaders called on the federal government to formalize their national boundaries. Chapter 4 uses a case study of a 1797 boundary survey to explain how clear borders offered a powerful mechanism for Cherokee and Chickasaw peoples to resist the invasion of their land. The new bordered landscape disrupted speculators' ongoing attempts to commodify Native territory, facilitated the identification of illegal white squatters, and enabled federal troops to evict intruders periodically from Cherokee and Chickasaw land beginning in 1798.

Drawing borders was not the only way Native inhabitants of the Tennessee Country adapted their geographical understandings of space and territory to defend their land from American expansionists. Chapter 5 analyzes how Cherokees and Chickasaws reimagined their nations' transportation networks for their own benefit and how these projects revealed the paradoxes of early U.S. state power. The early federal state reached into Native nations, but the ability of Cherokees and Chickasaws to shape the operation of U.S. state power limited Americans' imperialist goals. Chapter 6 investigates the competing geographies between Cherokees and Chickasaws, as members of both nations employed conflicting strategies to defend their territory from the growing American empire of the early nineteenth century. Chickasaws more often argued that their nation possessed land outright, whereas Cherokees insisted that much of the Tennessee Country was the shared hunting territory of all Indigenous southerners. Their dispute provides a window into a complex legal conversation about differing notions of space and territory, a conflict generated by U.S. expansion but occurring within Native America. The book concludes by exploring the legacy of American empire and Indigenous geographies for contemporary inhabitants of the Tennessee Country. *Marking Native Borders* is not a declension narrative of Chickasaw and Cherokee dispossession. Rather, it reveals Native peoples' creative adaptations and powerful persistence against the forces of American empire, strategies that began in the eighteenth century and continue to influence the competing geographies of the Tennessee Country in the present day.

Note on Terms

Given the power and contemporary relevance of Native sovereignty and American empire, I must clarify how I describe Tennessee Country inhabitants. I use "nation" to designate Indigenous polities, following historians' conclusions that terms like "band" and "tribe" denigrate Native peoples with their connotations of cultural inferiority, that Native southerners themselves often identified as members of larger collective units, and that eighteenth- and nineteenth-century Americans also employed "nation" to describe Indigenous polities when speaking of them on equal terms.[17] I apply the designations "Native" and "Indigenous" to Native Americans, and I capitalize these terms because they represent a person's national status. I avoid the term "Indian" except when drawing on information from primary sources, and I refrain from using Eurocentric titles such as "king" or "emperor," which European and American diplomats often imposed on Native leaders.[18]

When I reference specific Indigenous individuals, I employ the name that most often appears in the documentary record. If this is an English name or a translation from the Cherokee or Chickasaw language, I add a transliteration of the Indigenous name in parentheses when I first mention the individual. I record any alternate names in parentheses as well, given that Native individuals' names could change or might differ based on specific contexts.[19]

I frequently apply the racial designation "white" to distinguish non-Native individuals from African Americans and Native Americans. Although concepts of race evolved over time, most inhabitants of the Tennessee Country applied this description of phenotypic difference for people of European descent.[20] Scholars debate the utility of "settler," because, as historian Andrew Fitzmaurice notes, the term seemingly ignores Native sovereignty with the connotation that settlers were "people who occupy land that previously belonged to nobody."[21] Nevertheless, I use "settler" to describe white, non-Native residents of the Tennessee Country because of the term's connection to the process of settler colonialism.

Chapter 1

Straight Paths and Bordered Lands in the Eighteenth-Century Tennessee Country

In May 1767, Ostenaco (Jud's Friend), an experienced Cherokee diplomat and war leader from Tomotley, traveled east from his home in the Tennessee Valley to the banks of the Tyger River in the foothills of the Blue Ridge Mountains. He arrived there on June 1 alongside thirty-eight other Cherokee women and men. The purpose of the Cherokees' trip, as one Native negotiator understood it, was to create "a straight path" with British officials, including William Tryon, governor of North Carolina, and Cherokee commissary Alexander Cameron. For Native southerners, straight paths symbolized peaceful, stable diplomatic relationships.[1] The Cherokees' declaration of a new straight path, therefore, spoke to the potential for future peace with Great Britain and the colony of North Carolina.

Yet in this instance the path was much more than a metaphor. For nearly two weeks, the Cherokees and British agents marked a border on the landscape from Reedy River to the top of either Tryon or Whiteoak Mountain—a fifty-three-mile portion of a boundary line negotiated in prior treaty conferences. Though they had insisted on this extension of their border into North Carolina, having identified most of the South Carolina boundary a year before, the assembled Cherokees still found the survey a traumatic experience. Native peoples had always understood their national boundaries, but creating a border "was a thing never done by any of his predecessors," explained one Cherokee surveyor. "His people . . . were Crying about it." Their grief stemmed from their permanent loss of land east of the new boundary, a significant "crisis of cosmology" that disrupted Cherokees' spiritual ties to the environment and hardly could be compensated by British goods. "The Price the white People give for Land when they buy," noted Ostenaco upon beginning the survey, "is very small, they give a shirt, a match Coat and the like which soon wear out but Land lasts always." Fortified by promises from British officials, Cherokees had faith that the new border would limit white encroachment on their nation. With the towering Blue Ridge Mountains now serving as a natural and seemingly permanent border between the Cherokee Nation and North Carolina, Ostenaco cheered the successful survey. The "Line is now done" and "the Mountains stand for a Boundary for ever, as they will never wear out." With the survey, Cherokee diplomats inscribed their imagined geography onto the land by dividing Native space from that of the British Empire.[2]

International boundary lines may have been relatively new to Native diplomats in 1767, but Cherokees and Chickasaws repeatedly defined their national limits in subsequent confrontations with growing numbers of white invaders. In nearly every interaction with Anglo-Americans between 1767 and 1783, Cherokees and Chickasaws demanded that whites recognize their nations' borders and often threatened to drive intruders from their lands by force. Native peoples, British administrators, local settlers, and American officials negotiated and fought over Tennessee Country lands, and, in doing so, they revealed their own imagined geographies and future goals for the region. Rather than a simple contest between Indigenous peoples and white colonists, the late eighteenth century witnessed a kaleidoscopic struggle for control of the Tennessee Country.

As various groups defended their geographical visions, they experienced unanticipated political, legal, and diplomatic changes that would have lasting consequences for the region's history. Cherokees' and Chickasaws' political cultures were interconnected with their imagined geographies. Partisan infighting, regional polarity, generational disputes, clan ties, and gender divisions all influenced Native peoples' responses to whites' colonization of the Tennessee Country. Members of each nation disagreed about international alliances, prioritized their town's or region's interest above all else, favored greater political representation for younger leaders, and employed cultural conceptions of femininity and masculinity for diplomatic gain. Throughout the 1770s and 1780s, Chickasaws and Cherokees navigated these internal fissures to defend their territory, sovereignty, and property collectively, even if they disagreed on the best way to protect their lands from white invaders.

Indigenous geographies also shaped the relationship between white stakeholders of the Tennessee Country and distant colonial, state, and national governments. The European settlers who first colonized the region in the 1760s and 1770s sought liberty and independence that stemmed from unfettered access to North America's vast continental interior. These goals were similar to those of their eastern counterparts debating the merits of rebellion against Great Britain and clamoring for absolute, allodial ownership of real property.[3] White intruders romanticized Indigenous territory as vacant land, ripe for the taking. In practice, however, Chickasaws and Cherokees disrupted settler expansion, both militarily and diplomatically, and generated a continual political reorganization among white colonists as they attempted to perfect a settler empire in the Tennessee Country.

The Tennessee Country before European Invasion

The Tennessee Country has always been Native land, though it was a region experiencing major changes at the beginning of European colonization of North America. Many of the large, centralized Mississippian chiefdoms of the American South had begun to fragment by the mid-1500s, a process that accelerated after regular contact with colonial violence brought by the Spanish, French, and English. European diseases like smallpox, influenza, and yellow fever resulted in the deaths of thousands, and the massive population loss limited Indigenous peoples' ability to oppose European invasions. The expanding Indian slave trade only added to the upheaval of the seventeenth-century Native South. Out of this "shatter zone"—a term coined by anthropologist Robbie Ethridge to describe the dramatic collapse of the Mississippian chiefdoms—coalesced new, more egalitarian societies that were connected by kinship ties, cultural practices, and linguistic similarities. Among these were the Chickasaws, speakers of a Muskogean language who formed communities along the headwaters of the Tombigbee River after the decline of the Chicaza chiefdom. The Cherokee people were another coalescent society. Speakers of an Iroquoian language, Cherokees organized themselves into at least five groups of culturally related towns located along the Little Tennessee, Hiwassee, Keowee, Tugaloo, Oconaluftee, and Tuckasegee Rivers and their tributaries.[4]

By the early eighteenth century, imperial rivalries between France, Spain, and Great Britain for control of North America had brought trade and additional violence to the Chickasaws and Cherokees. Leaders of the two Indigenous nations cultivated diplomatic ties with the British colonies of South Carolina and Virginia. The Chickasaws were a useful ally. Their location in the Mississippi Valley hindered French officials from linking Louisiana and New France, and Chickasaw forces successfully resisted several invasions by French soldiers and their Choctaw allies between 1736 and 1752 before making peace with the

Choctaws in 1759. Several hundred Chickasaws even moved east to the Savannah River, closer to British trade and away from French attacks. Chickasaws and Cherokees often believed that their national interests aligned with those of British officials and their valuable trade goods, though Cherokees, in particular, did not recognize exclusive trading relationships and often cultivated alternative connections with other European colonies and Indigenous peoples.

The Seven Years' War had dramatic implications for both nations. In the beginning of this global conflict, Cherokees and Chickasaws fought with British forces against France and its Native allies. Yet, by late 1758, Cherokees went to war against Great Britain, a decision caused by Virginians' murder of Cherokees, ongoing encroachment by South Carolina colonists, and Cherokees' diplomatic and trading difficulties with Native peoples of the Ohio Valley. Before making peace three years later, Cherokees lost a third of their population to the combined ravages of sickness, famine, and British raids, which occasionally included Chickasaw soldiers. Great Britain's victory over the French in 1763, however, initially appeared to serve Cherokee and Chickasaw interests, even if Native peoples could no longer manipulate the competing empires against one another. Imperial officials cordoned off most of the continental interior of North America with the Proclamation of 1763, which outlawed settlement and speculation west of the Appalachian Mountains and made colonists' purchase of Native land illegal. The Proclamation reflected new spatial dimensions of empire among British officials, who believed that effective governance of their American colonies depended on separating British subjects from Indigenous peoples.[5] In major diplomatic negotiations between 1763 and 1774, Native diplomats from across North America codified their eastern borders with Britain's American colonies in accordance with the Proclamation Line.

For the Cherokees and Chickasaws, this process began in November 1763. Representatives from both nations traveled to Augusta, Georgia, where they met with John Stuart, Britain's superintendent of Indian affairs for the Southern Department, as well as diplomats from the Choctaw, Creek, and Catawba Nations and governors of the four southern colonies. Chickasaws and Cherokees used the opportunity to advocate for stable trading relationships with Britain. Attakullakulla (Little Carpenter)—the most senior regional leader, or "beloved man," and a chief diplomat for Cherokees of the Tennessee Valley—sanctioned existing white settlements in South Carolina but insisted that the New River be the Cherokee Nation's northern boundary with Virginia. Stuart later noted that Cherokees hoped "that the intermediate Space, between their Towns, and the

Map of the Southern Indian District, 1764. Archives and Special Collections, University of Pittsburgh Library System. The "Cherokee Hunting Ground" includes territory north of Cherokee towns along the Tennessee River and its tributaries.

back Settlements of the Carolinas might remain vacant." In addition to clear boundary lines, Cherokees preferred buffer zones of hunting land around their nation to better protect their territorial sovereignty. Stuart's map of the Southern Indian District from the Treaty of Augusta designated a large swath of territory north of the Holston River as "Cherokee Hunting Ground," a cartographic representation of Cherokees' imagined geographies.[6]

However, subsequent negotiations between British and Cherokee diplomats—including the 1767 survey of North Carolina's western boundary—more often resulted in land cessions. Cherokee leaders from across the nation insisted that their international borders "must be very evident" in order to prevent white encroachment. Nevertheless, the 1768 Treaty of Hard Labour and the 1770 Treaty of Lochaber only accelerated intrusion. Colonial officials pressured Cherokees for these treaties at the behest of Virginia speculators, who wanted access to the Ohio Valley and hoped to include recent settlements along the upper Holston River within the colony.[7] Thus, the actual creation of boundaries between British colonies and Indigenous nations was much more contentious and complex than the passage of the Proclamation of 1763 might suggest. Colonial officials balanced British subjects' demands for western land with acknowledgments of Native sovereignty. Cherokees remained in control of their expansive hunting territory in the Tennessee Country, but ongoing revisions to their nation's borders jeopardized their permanent access to the valuable land.

The Watauga Association and Overhill Diplomacy

While speculators pressured colonial officials for treaty negotiations, white settlers were already crossing the Appalachian Mountains into the upper reaches of the Tennessee Valley by the late 1760s, taking little notice of Native boundary lines. They established small farms and homesteads along the Watauga, Nolichucky, and Holston Rivers. Many of these early settlers hoped to take advantage of the growing economic opportunities in the West, like the fur trade, cheap land, and rich resources of wild game. When whites began moving into the region, they assumed that they were living within Virginia and therefore subject to its laws, including a provision that granted four hundred acres to anyone who erected a cabin and cultivated backcountry land. Once British officials surveyed the new boundaries of North Carolina, Virginia, and the Cherokee Nation in 1771, however, settlers could no longer plead ignorance to living in Native territory. British Indian agent Alexander Cameron ordered these settlers to leave the Cherokee Nation in 1772 in accordance with existing treaty agreements.[8]

White intruders ignored Cameron's orders and rejected Britain's constrictions on their settlement patterns. As British subjects, settlers knew that they could not legally purchase Native land, but they avoided the restriction by leasing land from Cherokee leaders in 1772. John Bean and James Robertson negotiated with Cherokees at Chota for a lease of territory along the Watauga River in exchange for annual payments in guns, blankets, liquor, and other goods. Jacob Brown secured a similar contract for settlers in the Nolichucky watershed. Cherokees understood these agreements as compensation for harvesting wild game only, not permission for permanent settlements. The Europeans, however, had other ideas. According to Brown, Cherokees were "the antient and undoubted owners" of their national territory and "had every natural and Equitable Right to dispose of Lands." Brown's agreement with the Cherokees, therefore, constituted a "purchase for which he paid them a valuable *bona fide* consideration." Whites easily recognized Native land ownership when it facilitated their access to Indigenous territory.[9]

In late 1772, British inhabitants of the Tennessee Valley established the Watauga Association to legitimize their property rights. Administered by a council of leading residents, Watauga existed as an independent government outside of any colony's jurisdiction. It was a true settler republic, directly responsive to its 1,500 inhabitants and committed to ongoing expansion. Almost immediately, the Watauga council organized militia companies and certified settlers' existing landholdings. Watauga residents furthermore made independent purchases of their homesteads from the Cherokee Nation in 1775. One indenture acknowledged that Cherokees were "the aborigines and sole owners by occupancy from the beginning of time" of territory along the Holston, New, and Watauga Rivers. Because the British Empire and colonial administrators refused to sanction their property rights, settlers, ironically, based their occupation on Natives' own historical ownership of the land.[10]

The Cherokees were not passive victims of colonists' deception. Between the Seven Years' War and the American Revolution, representatives from across the Cherokee Nation took part in treaty negotiations with British officials. Native diplomats from the Overhill Towns in the Tennessee Valley and from the Lower Towns along the Keowee and Tugaloo Rivers in present-day South Carolina were especially prominent. Select leaders of the Middle, Valley, and Out Towns, living along the headwaters of the Little Tennessee and Hiwassee Rivers in the Great Smoky Mountains, frequently joined them. Cherokee governance and diplomacy at this time was primarily a local matter. These regional groups of Cherokee towns shared a similar culture and language but often acted with relative independence of one another. In the coming decades, Cherokees would become more centralized to better defend their national lands. Nevertheless, Cherokees' decentralized, town-based government impacted their strategic defense of national territory and shaped the early white settlement of the upper Tennessee Valley.[11]

Regional leaders often dealt with white encroachment on their towns' hunting land. As early as 1769, Oconostota (Great Warrior), Attakullakulla, Kittagusta (Prince of Chota), Savanukeh (The Raven of Chota), and other Overhill diplomats and war leaders negotiated with nearby white intruders because their settlements threatened Overhill hunting territory and meant a decrease in wild game. They complained to British officials of the intruders' lack of regard for Cherokee sovereignty and property rights, well aware that the upper Tennessee Valley belonged to their nation and had been confirmed in treaty agreements. "The white people pay no Regard to all our Talks," protested Oconostota and Attakullakulla to Superintendent Stuart in 1769, "but do as they please for they Steal our deer and Land." At the conference leading to the Treaty of Lochaber, Attakullakulla feared that "in two Years more . . . the White people would Settle quite up to their doors." The Overhills were especially incensed that the Long

Island of the Holston, a site of great spiritual and diplomatic significance for the entire nation, was "full of White Hunters and the Guns rattling every way." It was so important to Cherokee interests that during the Lochaber boundary survey in 1771 Attakullakulla agreed to cede territory all the way to the Kentucky River in exchange for permanent control over the Long Island.[12]

By 1776, however, Overhill Cherokees realized that Watauga settlers had no interest in respecting Native property rights. "We suffered the people who first settled themselves on our land on Watauga to remain there some years, they paying us annually in guns, blankets and rum," Savanukeh explained to the Cherokees' Indian agent. Having heard that the Watauga settlers "gave out publicly that we sold the land to them forever," Savanukeh, whose town's hunting territory abutted whites' homesteads, wanted the British to make the colonists "move to some other land within the white people's bounds." Overhills felt similarly regarding the 1775 Treaty of Sycamore Shoals, a notorious agreement with North Carolina speculator Richard Henderson that opened 20 million acres in Kentucky for his Transylvania Land Company in exchange for a pittance in trade goods. Old Tassel (Onitositah) later charged that Henderson was "a rogue and a liar" for forging Oconostota's signature on the treaty. He insisted that Cherokee leaders had agreed only that Henderson should "have a little lands on Kentucky river, for his cattle and horses to feed on." They had not intended to give up their access to so much valuable territory.[13]

The Overhills' disgust with Watauga inhabitants and the Treaty of Sycamore Shoals stemmed, in part, from differing geographical understandings among Cherokees and white settlers and speculators. Cherokees willingly had shared their hunting land with nearby British colonists in exchange for goods. Overhills likely intended that their agreements with Henderson and Watauga settlers would incorporate their white neighbors into existing Indigenous territorial systems, where land was most often shared among groups rather than claimed outright. When colonists insisted on their allodial ownership rights, they disrupted Cherokees' property conceptions. Overhill leaders were anxious upon seeing Henderson at subsequent treaty negotiations because his presence symbolized this incompatibility. One Native diplomat was reluctant to sign future treaties because Henderson "had deprived Him of the privilege of catching even Craw fish on the land." Whites' insistence that they were the exclusive owners of Tennessee Valley land not only made Cherokee territory inaccessible but also broke from Cherokee cultural norms.[14]

Cherokees' response to white intrusion had lasting internal and external diplomatic implications. Internally, it sparked political disputes within the Cherokee Nation over notions of gender and masculinity. Although older Cherokee leaders most often acted as the nation's diplomats, younger men frequently attended treaty negotiations and resented territorial cessions to British colonists. By 1769, Attakullakulla, Oconostota, and other Overhill leaders were already warning British officials that "our young Fellows are very angry to See their Hunting Grounds taken from them." Oconostota worried about how to respond to younger men returning from annual hunts, who would ask "why should these Old men give away the Land without our knowledge." Younger Cherokee men resented land cessions made by older leaders because they needed the Cherokees' vast hunting territory, where they could prove their masculinity and harvest game for sustenance and the deerskin trade. Older leaders, however, were secure in their masculinity and relied on the distribution of trade goods to preserve their political power. Their prominent roles in diplomacy only increased their masculine status, even when they agreed to cede land.[15]

Such intergenerational conflict came to a head during Cherokee negotiations at the Treaty of Sycamore Shoals. Although Attakullakulla, Oconostota, and Savanukeh took the lead in negotiations, they were joined at the conference by Dragging Canoe (Tsi-yugunsini), Attakullakulla's son and the head warrior of Mialquo, a Cherokee town located on an island in the Little Tennessee River. During the second day of negotiations, Dragging Canoe stormed out of the conference after realizing that Henderson wanted the Overhills to make yet another land cession, though not before threatening that Kentucky would "be dark, and difficult to settle," it being "bloody Ground." Dragging Canoe's opposition to white intruders led him to accept a war belt from a visiting delegation of Shawnees, Delawares, Mohawks, and other Ohio Valley Native peoples only a year later. He and many young warriors painted themselves black in preparation for raids on British settlers. Demonstrating the intersection of gender, politics, and spatial organization, Dragging Canoe would later lead many younger Cherokee "warrior-diplomats" in establishing new towns south of the Overhill settlements along Chickamauga Creek, a tributary of the Tennessee River. For the next two decades, leaders of these communities—known as the Chickamauga Cherokees—would become the most militant opponents of ongoing white expansion in the Tennessee Country even as they exercised significant political power within the Cherokee Nation as a whole.[16]

As for changing external relations, Cherokees leveraged their diplomatic ties with Great Britain to isolate Watauga settlers from colonial officials. Great Britain needed to maintain good relations with Indigenous peoples in light of political upheaval throughout North America. John Stuart and Josiah Martin, North Carolina's colonial governor, both demanded that Watauga residents relocate elsewhere. Stuart and Britain's Cherokee agent, Alexander Cameron, even sent a party of Cherokees to warn off the white residents in 1774, demonstrating the close connection between British and Cherokee interests. The Watauga Association did not have the support of British officials, who deemed it to be "a dangerous example to the people of America, of forming governments distinct from and independent of his majesty's authority." The survival of the Watauga Association set a serious precedent at a time when British officials were already struggling to maintain control over their American colonies.[17]

Dependence and Defined Borders

Wataugans abandoned their tenuous independence in favor of dependence on the state of North Carolina. In 1776, Tennessee Valley whites lobbied North Carolina's Provincial Congress—recently organized to promote separation from Great Britain—to annex the upper Tennessee Valley. The 111 signers of the annexation petition promised to respect the Continental Congress and contribute to the "glorious cause of Liberty." Knowing their unruly reputation might give pause to eastern rebel leaders, Wataugans insisted that they had formed an orderly government; they were not a "lawless mob." Jacob Brown of the Nolichucky settlements made explicit the connection between annexation and settlers' property rights. In his personal petition to distant North Carolina leaders, Brown explained that he suffered great property losses from "the Ravages of the Indians." If he should be further "deprived of his Property in Lands and settlements" he would face "utter ruin." He wanted Watauga to be governed by North Carolina so that his "Title to such Lands . . . may be confirmed to him." Wataugans willingly surrendered some of their local sovereignty to the new state government and in turn expected state leaders to sanction their property rights and facilitate further colonization of Native land.[18]

Their desire to join North Carolina made sense in light of ongoing historical developments. Since North Carolina's reorganization as a royal colony in 1729, British administrators had dictated the terms of white Carolinians' relations with their Native neighbors. The state's rejection of British rule meant that eastern leaders were no longer beholden to the Indian policy of their imperial over-lords. Many believed that North Carolina would benefit by extending the state's jurisdiction over the Tennessee Valley because the area's white settlers could safeguard eastern settlements from Native attacks and act as valuable allies in the conflict with Great Britain. Legislators annexed the Watauga settlements in October 1776 during North Carolina's Fifth Provincial Congress, the same body that drafted the state's first constitution. They organized the region as the Washington District, a designation already in use by settlers to honor General Washington as the commander of the Continental Army.[19]

In 1776, therefore, Tennessee Valley whites' and eastern North Carolinians' interests aligned: they needed one another in their attempt to overthrow Brit-ish rule. Fear of Britain's Indigenous allies convinced Tennessee Valley settlers to make common cause against British and Native forces. Most famously, they contributed to the American victory at the Battle of Kings Mountain in 1780. Settlers appropriated the Revolutionary War to suit their own visions of the Tennessee Valley, turning the conflict into a war of conquest to secure their landholdings within the Cherokee Nation. They racialized local Loyalists as "white Indians," and, alongside Virginia troops, their militia razed thirty-six Cherokee towns and surrounding farmlands in the summer and fall of 1776. This campaign became all the more devastating because of concurrent inva-sions against Lower, Middle, Out, and Valley Towns by North Carolina forces, which created a refugee crisis within the Cherokee Nation. State leaders encour-aged white expansion in the Cumberland Valley by issuing land grants between the river and the Virginia line as payment for North Carolina troops and by allowing the small community of white settlers, who began to establish their fledgling community near present-day Nashville in the early 1780s, to maintain possession of their homesteads. Though it would take several decades for this region's population to equal that of the Tennessee Valley, surveying and specu-lating were avenues for political power in the eighteenth-century Cumberland settlements.[20]

Yet, as historian Jessica Choppin Roney points out, the new political arrange-ment between westerners and distant North Carolina legislators was "fraught, filled with contradictory words and actions in regard to settlers' sovereignty and self-government."[21] State leaders had little interest in preserving Native sovereignty, but they refused to sanction the unchecked expansion demanded by western settlers because it threatened potential speculation in western land. Cherokees and Chickasaws, ironically, had a greater impact on North Carolina's

Indian policy than Tennessee Country whites during the American Revolution, a conflict supposedly intended to reject distant imperial rule in favor of more locally responsive governments.

Cherokee diplomats and state officials agreed to delineate and define spatial boundaries as a check on white settlers' expansionist goals with the 1777 Treaty of Long Island of the Holston. Negotiated in July on the banks of the Holston River, the treaty was the brainchild of Patrick Henry, governor of Virginia, who wanted to perpetuate his state's existing peace with the Cherokee Nation and to ensure Virginians' direct access to the Kentucky Country through the Cumberland Gap. Governor Richard Caswell of North Carolina agreed with Henry's request to appoint treaty commissioners, whom he hoped would succeed in "establishing a Peace and fixing a Boundary line between the Cherokee Indians and the white people."[22] Over the course of the week-long negotiation, the North Carolina, Virginia, and Cherokee commissioners all engaged in complicated conversations that defined their people's respective geographical limits within the Tennessee Country. In doing so, they laid the foundation for a diplomatic relationship that had little room for the interests of local white settlers.

Reflecting eighteenth-century Cherokees' decentralized governing structure, where kinship and regional ties outweighed any national political consensus, the conference included only Overhill diplomats. Although present, Attakullakulla and Oconostota were in declining health, so negotiations fell primarily to Savanukeh and Old Tassel. They were joined by other local leaders such as Pot Clay (Thatagulla) of Chilhowee Town, who traveled to the Long Island of the Holston to meet with the Virginia and North Carolina commissioners because the negotiations dealt with issues important to his local community. The only non-Overhill attendee was Chow-we-hah of the Valley Towns, there to "hear what should be done." He likely intended to report the Long Island treaty proceedings to Cherokees of the Middle, Valley, Out, and Lower Towns, who had negotiated peace with South Carolina and Georgia earlier in May. Ostenaco, Dragging Canoe, Lying Fish (Utsuta-gana), and Old Tassel's maternal nephew John Watts (Young Tassel/Kunoskeskie)—all hailing originally from the Overhill Towns—were conspicuously absent from the negotiations at the Long Island.[23] Their decision to stay away reflected their increasing hostility toward the United States. Because they were not there to provide their consent, these Chickamauga leaders would not consider themselves bound by any agreement made with Virginia and North Carolina commissioners.

Peace could come about only through clear borders. The Virginians pressured the assembled Cherokees for unimpeded access to the Cumberland Gap; North Carolina's delegation expected the Native leaders to recognize their state's jurisdiction over all white settlers as far south as the Nolichucky River. Cherokees, too, favored "a firm and lasting Boundary," though one that included all of the Nolichucky and part of the Watauga watersheds within their nation. Providing a glimpse into Cherokees' internal delineation of space, Savanukeh explained that white settlements infringed on the property rights of Cherokees from Chilhowee and Settico, who "have their Hunting grounds chiefly up" the Nolichucky River. Inhabitants of these towns would "be verry thankful" if he could report that white settlers "are to be removed." Cherokee towns possessed rights to specific hunting territory, which white hunters disrupted. Eventually the Cherokee delegates agreed to cede Tennessee Valley territory encompassing all existing American settlements to the two states and grant Virginians a road to the Cumberland Gap. Their acceptance possibly related to Americans' promises of two hundred head of cattle and one hundred sheep plus future presents.[24]

Yet neither state treaty—both signed on July 20, 1777—was a victory for white expansionists. North Carolina and Virginia negotiators intended the agreements to create order in the Tennessee Country, not facilitate further colonization of Native land. North Carolina commissioners insisted that Cherokees should no longer "sell rent or make any agreement whatsoever, with private persons respecting the Lands on your side of the line." It was not just that these local land sales generated conflict between Cherokees and area settlers; North Carolina legislators had already outlawed all private land transactions with Native peoples in the state's constitution, with the 1777 treaty being the first application of the restriction. Commissioners questioned the validity of settlers' property in the Washington District. The North Carolina treaty recognized only state ownership of the region's territory, without referencing settlers' rights. Local whites likely were incensed further that the treaties prohibited any American from clearing land, hunting, or even herding cattle in the Cherokee Nation "on pain of being drove off by the Indians and his Property of every kind taken from him." When Savanukeh subsequently informed North Carolina governor Caswell that the "people of Wataugah . . . are marking trees all over my country, and near to the place I love, and are killing my stock near my beloved towns," Caswell issued a proclamation that officially invalidated intruders' title to stolen Native land in accordance with the state's Cherokee treaty and a recent act of North Carolina's general assembly.[25] In a war for property, the distant edicts of North

Carolina leaders must have come as quite a shock to many Washington District residents, who had sacrificed the political independence of the Watauga Association to join a state they thought sympathized with their expansionist agenda.

The ongoing Revolutionary War, however, offered American and Native dissidents a pretext for further localized violence over control of the Tennessee Country. Even as Overhill Cherokees negotiated peace along the Holston River, Dragging Canoe and his growing number of followers living along Chickamauga Creek attacked American settlers in Georgia, South Carolina, and Virginia's Kentucky counties. Chickamaugas cultivated ties with Great Britain for arms and trade goods to perpetuate their nearly incessant raids against white intruders. They welcomed anti-American Shawnees, Creeks, and even some British Loyalists into their new towns, creating a multiethnic community united in opposition to the United States. Virginia and North Carolina officials organized a preemptive raid against Chickamauga communities in 1779 and a much larger campaign in late 1780, which drove Chickamaugas farther down the Tennessee River, where they coalesced into five central towns by the mid-1780s. A force of seven hundred Tennessee Valley whites specifically targeted the Overhill Cherokees, despite the existing Long Island peace treaties. Nancy Ward (Nan-ye-hi), who held the title of war woman because of her participation in military exploits, and other Overhill officials attempted to forestall the attack, but they had little effect on militia officers. Americans suffered only three casualties during their invasion of the Cherokee Nation, allowing Arthur Campbell, a militia colonel from Washington County, Virginia, to cheer the destruction wrought on Overhill communities. He bragged to Governor Thomas Jefferson that the body of Virginia and North Carolina militia had razed eleven Native towns, captured over a thousand horses, and burned around fifty thousand bushels of corn. Campbell's force retreated before reaching the Chickamauga settlements, but he threatened to return unless Cherokee leaders agreed to negotiate yet another peace treaty.[26]

Organized by General Nathanael Greene, the commander of the Southern Department of the Continental Army, this new negotiation in the summer of 1781 was of national significance for both the United States and the Cherokee Nation. Greene had called for a peace conference with the Cherokees in the early months of 1781 while fighting a series of battles against General Cornwallis's British army in the Carolina backcountry. Greene's forces could ill afford an attack from across the Appalachians. Peace with Native southerners was a war measure. The American commissioners made sure to notify Cherokees that they were negotiating on behalf of the entire United States, not just Virginia and North Carolina. Yet, unlike the earlier Cherokee treaties of 1777 made by envoys from distant state governments, the U.S. treaty commission included Arthur Campbell, John Sevier, Joseph Martin, and Evan Shelby, all Tennessee Valley militia officers. Their presence ensured that negotiations would reflect settlers' expansionist agenda. Rather than regional and town-based representation, as had been the case in earlier treaties, the Cherokee delegation included representatives from a cross-section of their nation, including leading Cherokee women.[27] And, indeed, the American commissioners encountered spatial interpretations from this diverse Cherokee embassy.

Although the Chickamaugas had ignored the Overhill's previous peace agreements, the 1781 treaty conference revealed how the breakaway towns remained an important part of the Cherokee Nation. Overhills acted as the primary speakers, but they were joined by representatives from at least three Chickamauga towns, whom Oconostota described as "my own Nation and people." Rather than blame Chickamaugas for the past four years of violence, Oconostota weaved a narrative of whites' duplicity. Americans had never surveyed the 1777 boundary, and he believed "the People living near it would rather encroach [on the land] than run the Line." Cherokee hunting parties, composed primarily of young men like those flocking to Chickamauga towns, had repeatedly encountered white intruders in the upper Tennessee Valley. Such constant conflict over hunting land encouraged Cherokees "to go and Revenge the Thefts and Encroachments committed on our Lands." American hunters destroyed Cherokee property. "The wild Beasts in the Woods, are ours for us to live on," Au-koo of Chota reminded the U.S. commissioners. "Your game are Tame but ours a[re wi]ld, and hard to find." Younger men in attendance were encouraged that elder diplomats seemed committed to preserving their Tennessee Country hunting territory. They pledged to "listen no more to the English" and respect the negotiated peace.[28]

The most striking articulation of Cherokees' imagined geographies came from Native women. Cherokee society was matrilineal and matrilocal. Cherokee children became members of their mothers' clans and understood their identity in relation to their maternal kin network. A husband had little authority over his children, who were primarily raised by maternal uncles. Cherokee women's cultural prominence contributed to their political power over regional and national issues. For much of the seventeenth and eighteenth centuries, they organized separate councils from men and often influenced Cherokee decisions about war and peace. The Cherokees' discussions in 1781 were so significant for the nation that women demanded that they communicate with the American commissioners. Likely led by Nancy Ward, the women spoke through Oconostota and emphasized the gendered dimensions of Cherokee geography. "We are mothers, and have many Sons, Some of them Warriors, an[d] beloved Men," they began. "We call you also our sons," speaking directly to the U.S. commissioners. "We have a [r]ight to call you so, because you are the sons of Mothers, and all descended from the same Woman at first. We say you are our Sons because by women, you were brought forth into this world, nursed suckled, and raised up to be Men befo[re] you reached your present Greatness." By establishing this shared humanity, the Cherokee women were then able to ask, "Why should there be any Difference amongst us, we live on the same Land with you, and our People are mixed with white Blood." They envisioned a Tennessee Country where whites and Cherokees could access the region's resources in peace. Kinship, both fictive and real, already tied the two peoples together, so "why then will you quarrel with us," they asked the U.S. officials.[29]

After a week of negotiation, the American and Native treaty commissioners agreed on peace between the two nations. The settler-diplomats did not, however, embrace Cherokees' imagined geography. In his reply to the Cherokee women, William Christian acknowledged that he "was affected by" their talk, but he nevertheless insisted that peace would be possible only if Cherokees would "be still and quiet at Home." He had no intention of sharing the Tennessee Valley with Cherokee hunters or accepting their equality based on shared kinship. At least one commissioner had even planned to press the Cherokees for a land cession as punishment for recent attacks, though the conference concluded without such a transfer. White and Native delegates merely reconfirmed exiting boundary lines, organized a prisoner exchange, and arranged for another conference to take place later in the year. Commissioners also promised to enforce Cherokee borders by removing white intruders.[30]

Both sides emphasized their desire for peace, but localized violence broke out only months after the negotiations and continued for the next two years. With the exception of an attack on Cherokee towns in northern Georgia by South Carolina forces, the conflict mainly consisted of minor raids between Chickamaugas and individual militia companies. Notably, Governor Alexander Martin of North Carolina had hoped a militia campaign in 1782 would drive Chickamauga Cherokees from their new settlements back up the Tennessee Valley. "By confining and contracting their settlements," Governor Martin explained, Cherokees "will soon be circumscribed by white Inhabitants, and their power be reduced to the harmless and inoffensive situation of the Catawbas." Unlike the Catawbas, restricted to a reservation along North Carolina's border with South Carolina, Cherokees' dispersed settlements reinforced their sovereignty over the Tennessee Country and made them difficult to control, according to Martin.[31]

Chickasaw Peace, Chickasaw Power

Although nominally allied with Great Britain during the Revolutionary War, Chickasaws had pursued their own interests throughout the conflict. Similar to their actions before the war, they policed the Mississippi and Cumberland Rivers against U.S. and Spanish intruders and declared their loyalty to Great Britain. Prominent leaders threatened violence against Americans, and a group of Chickasaw raiders even attacked a U.S. fort constructed along the Ohio River in early 1781. After Spain drove Britain out of West Florida, however, Chickasaws began to disagree about the best diplomatic strategy. Wolf's Friend believed Chickasaws could be better served through closer ties to Spain, whereas Piominko looked to the United States. The nation's international diplomacy was further complicated by James Colbert, a Scottish trader living in Chickasaw territory, who led Loyalist refugees and some Chickasaws in raids against Spanish and French inhabitants in the Mississippi Valley without Native leaders' approval.[32]

Amid these complex internal and external developments, Chickasaw leaders aggressively pursued peace with the United States as their best strategy to maintain their sovereignty, a marked contrast to Chickamauga Cherokees, Creeks, and Shawnees, who continued fighting long after 1783. In July 1782, Payamataha, Mingo Houma, Tuskau Pautapau (The Red King), and Piominko notified American forces in the Kentucky Country that they wished "to Conclude a peace" on behalf of the Chickasaw Nation. Still facing potential conflict with Great Britain and ongoing attacks by Native peoples, Kentuckians enthusiastically embraced the opportunity to cultivate ties with the Chickasaws, long known for their military prowess. Although these Chickasaw leaders likely intended to negotiate a treaty with the entire U.S. government, Virginia exercised jurisdiction over Kentucky, and the state's governor, Benjamin Harrison, worked quickly to take the Chickasaws up on their offer of peace. He appointed Joseph Martin, Isaac Shelby, and John Donelson as treaty commissioners, collected provisions for the negotiations, and consulted the state legislature about a possible purchase of the territory bounded by the Ohio, Tennessee, and Mississippi Rivers.[33]

The Chickasaw negotiations offered a potential model for interstate Native diplomacy. While asking Governor Martin of North Carolina to send representatives from his state, Harrison mentioned his wish "that some regular plan was fixed on by the Southern States for the regulation of Indian Affairs" with permanent commissioners from Virginia, North Carolina, South Carolina, and Georgia. Greater regional control, Harrison believed, would be a cheaper and more efficient method than each state guarding its own borders and might make it easier to prevent whites' ongoing invasion of Native land. Martin agreed about the shared interests of southern states. The federal government was already in the process of organizing a separate Indian department to coordinate Native diplomacy in the South, though it would be administered by Congress and not state leaders. Shared interests—namely access to Native land—offered a means to bind the United States together.[34]

Yet the Chickasaws' innocuous entreaty for peace in the Tennessee Country threated the ideological underpinnings of future U.S. expansion. Harrison worried about the precedent for a conventional purchase of Native land. Should Virginia commissioners succeed in acquiring Chickasaw territory, Harrison ordered them to "be extremely guarded in wording the deed, that no expression be introduced from which a plea may be made, of our quitting the claim we have to the Land as laying within our Charter and resting it on the Indian purchase." Buying land outright would acknowledge Chickasaws' original ownership of their national territory and endanger future American expansion. Harrison hoped instead to perpetuate the legal fiction of the Discovery Doctrine, an international principle that discredited Native sovereignty because of Indigenous peoples' perceived cultural, social, and religious inferiority when confronted by the seemingly superior European civilization at the moment of contact.[35] Harrison's conundrum foreshadowed a defining feature of U.S. Indian policy in the decades after independence: how could the new nation acquire Native territory when Indigenous peoples remained in control of North America's interior?

Chickasaw diplomats made Harrison's worries irrelevant, at least in the short run, by insisting that they would dictate peace terms, which centered on trade rather than land cessions. For several years, Americans had pestered Chickasaws to sell land between the Tennessee and Mississippi Rivers, but they repeatedly refused. The Native leaders complained of Virginia's demand for a land sale and mentioned that Cumberland Valley settlers were surveying Chickasaw hunting territory. The Chickasaw Nation needed all of its land for a growing population, and Chickasaws' past experiences had shown that "the white people where once they make a Settlement Spread over the Land like the Bears seeking for mast." It was imperative that Chickasaws refuse a cession or risk being completely overrun by American intruders. Yet they still hoped to cultivate ties with the United States. Trade goods had cemented Chickasaws' long relationship with Great Britain, and Native leaders wanted similar connections with the new nation.[36]

Chickasaw leaders reiterated these points when finally meeting the Virginia commissioners in November 1783 along the Cumberland River. Tuskau Pautapau insisted that white settlers stop hunting and settling in the Chickasaw Nation. He argued that such encroachment fomented conflict, and he feared that Chickasaws would be blamed should other Native soldiers attack white intruders. Piominko furthermore outlined his nation's boundary lines for the treaty commissioners. He made sure to mention that the Chickasaws claimed Tennessee Country territory up to the Ohio River, a clear challenge to Virginia's prior attempts to acquire a land cession near the junction of the Ohio and Tennessee Rivers. Chickasaws were in control throughout the negotiations. Virginians agreed to open trade with the Chickasaw Nation, and negotiators provided the assembled leaders gifts to symbolize the arrangement. In exchange, Joseph Martin wanted Piominko and Tuskau Pautapau to evict all "disorderly people" from the Chickasaw Nation, including a body of Delawares whom the commissioners blamed for recent attacks on Kentucky and Cumberland settlements. The pro-American Chickasaws easily agreed to the requirement, likely already aware that such inhabitants threatened their relationship with the United States and knowing that Americans lacked the ability to enforce the provision.[37] For Chickasaws, peace was power.

When Ostenaco returned to the Tennessee Country in 1767 after negotiating with British officials about the Cherokees' southeastern border, the region was a Native space. He likely shared news of the boundary survey with the other women and men of the Overhill settlements. Cherokees had lost a portion of their hunting land east of the Blue Ridge Mountains when making the survey, but Ostenaco was confident that the British would "permit no persons to settle on their Lands, and that no Hunters be allowed to . . . go on their Hunting Grounds."[38] Despite years of war with neighboring colonists, Cherokees could finally rest assured that their national sovereignty was secure. Yet even as these Cherokees created their nation's southeastern boundary in the late 1760s, white colonists were invading their nation in the northern reaches of the Tennessee Valley. The mountains were already more sieve than barrier, which became even more the case over the next several decades when the numbers of white intruders in Cherokee territory sky-rocketed. Ostenaco and the other Cherokee women and men soon learned that white settlers had their own ideas for the region, ideas that depended on the permanent displacement of Indigenous peoples.

Even with U.S. victory in the Revolutionary War, however, Chickasaws and Cherokees persisted against the forces of settler empire. Chickasaws dictated the terms of their nation's diplomatic relationship with the United States at a time when U.S. officials could ill afford further conflict, given the existing tension with Great Britain and its Native allies. They insisted that the new settler nation would acknowledge Chickasaws' right to Tennessee Country territory. Chickasaw leaders made clear that, even though they favored closer ties with the United States, they would make diplomatic decisions to secure their own national interests. Trade and sovereignty, rather than land cessions and white expansion, would structure U.S.-Chickasaw diplomacy for the foreseeable future.

Conflict, on the other hand, continued to undergird Cherokees' relations with their American neighbors. Cherokee lands remained under greater threat from the expanding settler empire than those of the Chickasaws. U.S. independence, ironically, had the potential to restructure relations between white Americans and Cherokees. Cherokee leaders and colonial officials had created a British-Cherokee boundary in the 1760s to create peace between the two peoples.[39] Along similar lines, some Cherokees now called on distant governments—both North Carolina and the United States—to check whites' invasion of their national lands in the 1780s, just as Ostenaco had done sixteen years earlier.

Chapter 2

Land Speculators, White Intruders, and the Beginnings of a "Great American Empire"

Chickasaws were frustrated in the summer of 1783. They had repeatedly contacted American officials about the need for diplomatic and trading relationships, but nothing tangible had come of their communications. Uncertain about evolving international developments, Mingo Houma, Piominko, Payamataha, and two other Chickasaw leaders sent a formal communique to the United States' Confederation Congress in July asking for clarification and action. Chickasaws explained that they were "daily receiving Talks from one Place or other, and from People we Know nothing about." These included Spain, a power with whom Chickasaws had long been familiar, but Mingo Houma, Piominko, and Payamataha also mentioned additional communications from Georgia and Virginia. They were aware that "the Americans have 13 Councils Compos'd of Chiefs and Warriors" but knew "not which of them we are to Listen to, or if we are to hear some, and Reject others." The Chickasaw leaders offered a solution to the disorder: greater congressional involvement in North America's interior. They would question the United States' legitimacy unless Congress initiated formal diplomatic and trading relations with the Chickasaw Nation. They called on Congress to "put a stop to any encroachments on our lands" and "silence those People who sends us Such Talks as inflame & exasperate our Young Men." Should Congress refuse to act, Chickasaws would pursue greater ties to Spain.[1] Successful negotiations with Virginia in November 1783 temporarily quelled the Chickasaws' irritation with the United States, but their demands exposed the growing uncertainty over control of the Tennessee Country in the aftermath of U.S. independence.

The 1780s witnessed ongoing and multifaceted attempts of local settlers, land speculators, and state governments to secure the region for white expansion.

Many western settlers still longed for a political system that could legitimize their ownership of stolen Native land and facilitate further colonization. The Watauga Association represented white settlers' first attempt at an expansionist, locally responsive government in the Tennessee Valley, but in 1784 the region's inhabitants created the State of Franklin, an extralegal regime that defied North Carolina rule. Although Franklin would ultimately disintegrate after failing to secure congressional recognition, the breakaway state government exemplified what political scientist Adam Dahl terms a "democratic empire," where white inhabitants "demanded territorial expansion as a necessary correlate of democratic equality and self-rule." In its short history, Franklin would make a lasting statement that local settlers, not distant governments or land speculators, should be the driving force of imperialism in the Tennessee Country.[2]

Speculators' commodification of Cherokee and Chickasaw land already deviated from settlers' expansionist goals, even as it also threatened Native sovereignty. After the American Revolution, North Carolina and Georgia legislators sold vast expanses of territory to offset their states' wartime debts, using victory over Great Britain to proclaim their right of conquest to the lands of Britain's Native allies. Conquest theory, a legal concept of growing importance in the eighteenth-century Atlantic World, held that a nation gained sovereignty over other nations through military victory. European empires, for example, frequently employed conquest theory after defeating Indigenous peoples, as exemplified by British claims to the territory of France's Native allies after the Seven Years' War. Many Americans maintained that victory over Great Britain similarly gave the United States rights of conquest over its Indigenous allies.[3] Notions of conquest were foundational for speculators' arguments that their state land grants were superior to the rights of Cherokees and Chickasaws in the Tennessee Country. These expansionist land claims created tension between speculators and the federal government, particularly after national leaders insisted that the United States had a right of preemption to Native land, meaning that only the United States could purchase territory from Indigenous peoples.[4]

U.S. officials' reluctance to support settlers and speculators attempting to craft an expansive American empire in the Tennessee Country was a direct result of Native power. Although many Americans blustered about their conquest rights to Indigenous territory in the early 1780s, Native peoples rejected such notions and frequently used violence to resist whites' encroachment. "The doctrine of conquest is so repugnant" to Indians, explained secretary of war Henry Knox, "that rather than submit thereto, they would prefer continual war."

Ongoing conflict in the trans-Appalachian borderlands convinced the Confederation government to return to the British model of negotiated land purchases through treaty agreements that recognized Indigenous sovereignty and checked settler expansion. U.S. leaders believed that treaties could better control frontier whites, who threatened national security, provoked conflict with Native nations, and appeared willing to embrace allegiance to European empires.[5] Cherokee and Chickasaw diplomats first experienced this new orderly relationship with the United States during negotiations at Hopewell Plantation in the final months of 1785. Growing U.S. involvement in the Tennessee Country provided Chickasaws and Cherokees with additional opportunities to defend their national lands by articulating their imagined geographies of the region.

"Get as Much Land as Possible"

While British and U.S. officials haggled over peace terms at the revolution's end, North Carolinians tried to put the American empire into practice by seizing Native land through legislative fiat. Since the 1770s, North Carolina officials had attempted to exercise stable governance over the Tennessee Country. State leaders had agreed to annex the settlements along the Watauga, Nolichucky, and Holston Rivers, but they insisted, at least in principle, that the local settlers respect Cherokees' borders. With debt mounting due to military expenses from the Revolutionary War, however, North Carolina legislators believed the state's western lands could generate much-needed revenue. They had already appropriated territory along the Cumberland River as payment for North Carolina troops, and, in May 1783, state leaders authorized almost all the land between the Mississippi River and Appalachian Mountains to be sold to white buyers through a land office located at Hillsborough, North Carolina. With the law, legislators commodified Native territory without consulting the Chickasaws and Cherokees, who exercised sovereignty over the region. This appropriation was possible because of the decentralized nature of the Articles of Confederation. State governments had the authority to administer Indian affairs within their constitutional borders. Yet it also aligned with white Americans' emerging understandings of conquest theory to justify their unilateral expansion onto Native land. Although North Carolina maintained existing diplomatic ties to the Cherokee Nation, the state militia's destruction of Cherokee towns in 1777 bolstered North Carolinians' claims of conquest.[6]

The 1783 law, grounded in notions that delegitimized Native peoples' land-ownership, allowed white North Carolinians to carve out property within the

Cherokee and Chickasaw Nations. Some speculators, like Richard Caswell, North Carolina's former governor and current speaker in the state senate, knew of the act's imminent passage and already had agents in place to identify the most valuable tracts of western land. Others organized separate surveying ventures, which "drove out parties of the Indians from their hunting grounds, and . . . caused a general alarm," according to one critic. Before the Hillsborough land office closed in May 1784, North Carolina speculators had entered more than three million acres.[7] As much as North Carolina governance had depended on controlling white settlers' expansionist aspirations in the Tennessee Country, legislators now created speculator property within the negotiated borders of the Chickasaw and Cherokee Nations, giving many easterners a personal stake in future expansion.

North Carolina officials not only commodified Native territory in 1783 but also claimed the authority to define Cherokee geography. The land law created a Cherokee reservation, bounded by the French Broad River to the north, the Tennessee River to the west, the Georgia state line to the south, and the Appalachian Mountains to the east. Governor Alexander Martin repeatedly contacted Cherokees in accordance with legislative dictates to gain their approval for the reservation in exchange for trade goods and gunpowder. Although Martin used language that seemingly acknowledged Cherokee sovereignty as the basis for speculators' property rights, he threatened military action against the Chickamaugas if they refused to move back into the territory reserved to them by the state. The potential for violence by what Martin termed "the great American Empire" underpinned North Carolina's appropriation of Indigenous land.[8] Cherokees never assented to this unilateral reduction in their nation's territorial boundaries.

Even as the legislature facilitated colonization via state law, a cadre of North Carolinians organized their own private project to benefit from Native dispossession in the Great Bend of the Tennessee River, the territory located north of the river's turn into present-day Alabama. The region had long been important to Native peoples for its abundant supply of wild game and fertile soil. Cherokees, Chickasaws, and Creeks had alternatively shared and fought over the Great Bend for the past century. White speculators likewise wanted access to these natural resources, but the region's allure also centered on its importance for commerce and communication. By acquiring the Great Bend, Americans could potentially bypass the hazardous Muscle Shoals in the Tennessee River or connect the Tennessee River with the Coosa River, providing residents of the upper Tennessee Valley with a more direct route to Gulf Coast markets than the tedious trip down the Tennessee to the Ohio and then down the Mississippi.[9]

The venture in land speculation began in early 1783 at the behest of William Blount. The Blounts—including William's brothers Reading, John Gray, and Thomas—were merchants and politicians from eastern North Carolina with a history of using their political connections to procure western lands. Their Great Bend project was no different. William Blount cultivated his existing relationships with North Carolina legislators to form the Tennessee Company, with its "Grand Object . . . to get as much land as possible." Over time, Blount and his eastern allies recruited John Sevier, Griffith Rutherford, and Waightstill Avery to the company, believing that their influence as Indian fighters would attract potential settlers already living in the Tennessee Country. Westerners' participation was so significant to the project that, in at least one instance, Blount publicized Anthony Bledsoe's involvement because of his popularity among Tennessee Country inhabitants, despite privately admitting that Bledsoe had never officially joined the Tennessee Company.[10] Fraud and intrigue, it seemed, were as integral to the commodification of Native space as issues of sovereignty and property rights.

The Tennessee Company benefitted from the competing geographies of the Great Bend. Blount and his associates knew that "the bent of the Tenessee [was] in Georgia, & several Indian nations between," making it essential to "purchase the sd. Lands from the Indians." Overhill Cherokees sold their claim to the Great Bend for £1,000 worth of trade goods at a July 1783 meeting at the Long Island of the Holston. They relied less on the region's game than did the Chickamauga Cherokees, Chickasaws, or Creeks, so Overhill Cherokees possibly saw the sale to land company representatives as a way to procure needed goods without giving up much in return. Georgia and South Carolina also possessed conflicting claims to this portion of the Tennessee Valley, a situation "very favourable to our Designs," rejoiced Blount to Joseph Martin. A title from either Georgia or South Carolina would legitimize their venture because the company "would settle the Country before the Dispute can be determined." It was perfectly acceptable, even preferable, for the Tennessee Company's property rights to precede Georgia or South Carolina jurisdiction.[11]

The Tennessee Company was well on its way to creating landed property out of Native territory by the end of 1784. In February, Blount petitioned the Georgia legislature to acknowledge the company's rights to the Great Bend. Georgia selected seven commissioners, including three members of the company itself, to investigate the region and issue land grants if they found the venture possible. At their first meeting later in the summer, the four commissioners present established Houston County to encompass the Great Bend and appointed themselves to county offices. They later proposed to open a land office at the Long Island of the Holston to entice Tennessee Valley inhabitants to the Great Bend.[12] Tennessee Company officials realized their project would be most successful by transforming the Tennessee River into a corridor of American settlement and embracing local settlers' expansionist goals. This venture would, however, become increasingly tenuous as the federal government, Native peoples, and local settlers all wrestled for control over the Tennessee Country in the mid-1780s.

The State of Franklin

North Carolina's appropriation of Cherokee and Chickasaw territory in 1783 and the Tennessee Company's subsequent attempt to secure the Great Bend were both orchestrated by distant speculators. Although Americans in the Tennessee Country took part as land agents, eastern politicians called the shots. This continued to be the case when the North Carolina legislature ceded its western land to the Confederation Congress in 1784, a decision that left the Tennessee Country seemingly under the jurisdiction of the federal government. National leaders had long wanted state governments to cede their western land claims, believing that doing so would eliminate potential conflict among states and tie the new nation together through a shared interest in controlled expansion. North Carolina legislators' decision, however, centered more on their personal financial interest than on a commitment to U.S. governance. Speculators from the state's eastern counties shepherded the cession bill through the general assembly, hoping their claims to the Tennessee Country would be better protected by the U.S. government. Other legislators supported the cession because it would eliminate North Carolina's costly defense of its settlers across the Appalachian Mountains. Westerners in the state legislature were split. Those involved in land speculation supported the cession, while those with less to gain financially opposed it.[13]

After learning of the cession, forty prominent Tennessee Valley settlers met at Jonesborough in Washington County in August 1784 and began to create yet another breakaway government, similar to the Watauga Association. These local leaders had supported the Cession Act because it gave them an excuse to take control of Indian affairs and secure their property rights in the region. They resented state officials' dictates against further expansion into the Cherokee Nation and worried that North Carolina's 1783 land law opened their homesteads to speculators, since few Tennessee Valley inhabitants possessed formal deeds for their property. Locals' political decisions remained intertwined with their property rights. Jonesborough delegates selected John Sevier as their body's temporary president. Sevier was initially lukewarm in his support of the separatist movement because of his connections with the Tennessee Company and other eastern land speculators, but he did recognize the benefits of local rule. Contemplating a possible union of the Tennessee Valley's Virginia and North Carolina settlements two years earlier, Sevier had emphasized that the region's white population had experienced "Many Difficulties & with the Loss of many Good Citizens . . . chiefly Occasioned by our Remote situation from the seats of Government." At the time, he proposed that white residents form a separate government more responsive to their needs. Tennessee Valley settlers shared Sevier's earlier sentiments. In December 1784, a majority of the assembled delegates decided to form an independent state government that they would call Franklin, so-named to encourage Benjamin Franklin to support their statehood movement at the federal level. They made this decision even after learning that Carolina legislators had repealed the 1784 Cession Act in response to public opposition against speculator interests and uncertainty over the status of North Carolina's surviving wartime debt.[14]

The Franklinites based their entire government around unrestrained access to Native land and its transformation into private property. In their minds, Americans would flock to their state now that it was controlled by a government that would "improve agriculture, perfect manufacturers, encourage literature and everything truly laudable." The panacea for community development was further expansion, verging on genocide. David Campbell, a future Franklin judge, reported to his brother across the state line in Virginia that "there are some [delegates] for immediately attempting the utter Extirpation of the Indians."[15] Many early leaders of the Franklin movement had taken part in campaigns against Cherokee towns during the Revolutionary War and wholeheartedly rejected Indigenous sovereignty over any of the Tennessee Country. In its short existence, the State of Franklin would become the model settler state, responsive to its inhabitants' expansive agenda. White residents of the upper Tennessee Valley were beholden no more to distant rule.

Even as Franklin leaders rejected Native sovereignty in founding their breakaway state, North Carolina officials attempted to control their citizens west of the mountains, laying bare the contradictory impulses of the two governments. Neither the general assembly nor Governor Martin had learned of Franklinites'

actions when legislators received word from Old Tassel of whites' ongoing invasion of the Cherokee Nation. The Overhill leader reminded Governor Martin of
his promise "to have your people taken off our grounds, but it is not yet done.
When one goes off two comes in his place." Despite their past bluster about
punishing Cherokees for not relocating to North Carolina's reservation, Martin
and state legislators listened to Old Tassel and ordered Tennessee Valley whites
to vacate Cherokee land. North Carolina would not take part in a war with the
Cherokees caused by its own citizens.[16]

Events in 1785 further revealed the growing conflict between North Carolina and the State of Franklin over property rights and local sovereignty. First
learning of the Franklin movement early in the year, Martin worked quickly to
challenge its legitimacy. In a communication to the region's white population, he
eviscerated the Tennessee Country government. Martin argued that the region's
residents already had sufficient control of their local affairs under state rule, that
the Franklin secession actually put local residents in greater danger of Indian
attacks, and that the "revolt" of the western counties was unconstitutional under
the 1776 North Carolina constitution. Yet the governor's comments about land
provide a more accurate representation of why Franklin posed such a threat to the
state's eastern leadership. "Every citizen should reap the advantage of the vacant
territory," Martin continued, "that the same should be reserved for the payment
of the public debts of the State." Although North Carolina's initial response to
Franklin appeared to support Cherokees' sovereignty claims, Martin and other
legislators intended to sell Cherokee and Chickasaw territory to pay the state's
debt. Franklinites had essentially stolen North Carolina property by claiming the
Tennessee Country for themselves.[17] Easterners objected to Franklinites' expansionist vision because it endangered their own investment in Native dispossession while increasing the likelihood of war with the Cherokee Nation.

Taking no heed of Martin's demands, Franklin's leaders devoted themselves
to Native dispossession on their own terms. North Carolina speculators had
hoped to corral Cherokees on a bounded reservation south of the French Broad
and Tennessee Rivers with the 1783 land law. Franklinites, however, organized
their own treaty with Overhill Cherokees to procure territory included in North
Carolina's Cherokee reservation. In June 1785, they coerced a select few Overhill leaders from Chota, Chilhowee, Talasee, and Settico to make a land cession
in what would become known as the Treaty of Dumplin Creek. This agreement gave the State of Franklin official jurisdiction over white families who

had previously settled illegally on Native land. Franklinites threatened further invasion if any Cherokees resisted. Cherokees later repudiated the Treaty of Dumplin Creek because none of the nation's most prominent leaders were present during negotiations, but for Franklinites it epitomized their expansionist visions for the Tennessee Country with unfettered access to Native territory. The new government soon began granting land, building forts, and organizing new county governments in the ceded territory along the Little River, policies designed to secure Franklin's control over the region.[18] So important was access to Cherokee land that negotiations at Dumplin Creek took place even before local leaders drafted Franklin's constitution.

Their decision to establish the State of Franklin supposedly symbolized Tennessee Country whites' rejection of distant North Carolina governance, but Franklinites' choice to essentially replicate their former state's constitution demonstrated that the breakaway government was little more than a local landgrab—Native dispossession under the guise of democratic rule. Nearly a year after their first formal declaration of independence, sixty-four Franklin delegates assembled in November 1785 at Jonesborough for a constitutional convention. A few attendees took the opportunity to propose a truly revolutionary system of government that would include universal male suffrage, a unicameral legislature, popular elections for state and county officials, a public university funded through taxation on agricultural products and land surveying fees, and freedom of the press, alongside strict religious requirements for officeholders. Delegates instead voted to enact the existing North Carolina constitution as their governing structure.[19] The majority of Franklin leaders preferred a government that would merely sanction their property rights and facilitate their ongoing invasion of the Cherokee Nation, not institute a more egalitarian political system.

The State of Franklin's survival ultimately depended on recognition by the United States. In May 1785, William Cocke arrived in New York to lobby the Confederation Congress to admit the extralegal state into the Union. On the critical ballot, Franklin fell short by two votes. American leaders possibly shared Thomas Jefferson's view that the Tennessee Valley government set a dangerous precedent for the new nation. Should Congress acknowledge the State of Franklin's legitimacy, Jefferson worried, "States will crumble to atoms by the spirit of establishing every little canton into a separate state."[20] This would be the closest Franklinites ever came to federal recognition, though it would not prevent many Tennessee Valley expansionists from devising new means to secure their property and protect their sovereignty as they laid the foundation for a settler empire in the Tennessee Country.

Negotiating National Boundaries

While Cocke campaigned for Franklin statehood, Congress was already organizing a series of treaty negotiations for the following winter, beginning an Indian policy that was as much in opposition to North Carolina speculators as to Franklin expansionists. U.S. officials invited representatives of the Cherokee, Chickasaw, and Choctaw Nations to Hopewell Plantation in Upcountry South Carolina in the winter of 1785–86 to negotiate for peace with federal treaty commissioners Joseph Martin, Benjamin Hawkins, and Andrew Pickens. Congress tasked Hopewell negotiators with "making peace with [Native southerners], receiving them into the favour & protection of the United States and removing as far as may be all causes of future contention or quarrels," even as Franklinites were creating a settler government premised on Native dispossession and local sovereignty.[21]

For Cherokees, the conference represented an important political coalescence during internal disorder. The early 1780s had been especially difficult for the Cherokee Nation because of the nearly constant American raids and a national famine. Although many Overhill, Middle, Out, and Valley Town inhabitants remained in their mountain communities along various tributaries of the Tennessee River, some Cherokees created new settlements farther away from white settlers. Chickamaugas had already coalesced into their five major towns of Nickajack, Long Island, Crow Town, Running Water, and Lookout Mountain. Lower Town Cherokees from the Keowee River watershed were also in the process of creating new communities along the Coosawattee, Conasauga, Oostanaula, and Etowah Rivers in present-day northern Georgia. Indeed, the site of the Hopewell conference was within view of the Cherokee town of Seneca, though as an American commissioner noted it was "at present a waste." Cherokee leaders from across these regions took part in negotiations, and they were joined by more than nine hundred Cherokee women, men, and children. The American commissioners attributed the huge delegation to the Cherokees' fear of further violence from Franklinites, though it may have stemmed from some individuals' wish to observe the negotiations and hold their leaders accountable for decisions. Nancy Ward, there in her capacity as war woman of Chota, attended at the behest of her town's "young warriors," men who feared their elderly leaders might cede more of the nation's hunting territory.[22] Younger men relied on Ward to represent their interests during the momentous deliberations because of Cherokee women's traditional authority over community territory as agriculturalists. Cherokees' Hopewell Treaty represented a moment of national diplomacy for the Cherokee Nation that transcended regional, generational, and gender divides.

The Chickasaw delegation at Hopewell was much smaller than that of the Cherokees but also revealed the potential for political unity through international diplomacy. Piominko was the most vocal Chickasaw negotiator and frequently spoke for his relative Satopia, also in attendance. Mingo Taski Etoka (Mingatushka/Hare-Lipped King), the third-named Chickasaw leader at the conference, was known for his close ties to Spanish Louisiana. Yet Piominko had himself represented the Chickasaw Nation in treaty negotiations with Spanish officials at Pensacola the year before.[23] Piominko, Taski Etoka, and Satopia therefore likely saw the Hopewell conference as another opportunity to manipulate non-Native powers against one another for Chickasaws' benefit.

Cherokee and Chickasaw diplomats made clear their national goals for the negotiations and seized on the opportunity to once again complain of Americans' invasion of the Tennessee Country. "The people of North Carolina," explained Old Tassel, "have taken our lands for no consideration, and are now making their fortunes out of them." Whites had settled within "nine miles from our towns" and had even surveyed property near his community. Cherokees knew that speculators coveted their national territory, and they demanded that the United States put a stop to it. Chickasaws similarly complained of white men raising cattle and horses in their nation and wished "they would go with their property to their own lands, and enjoy it."[24] In their separate negotiations, however, Chickasaws and Cherokees did more than complain of whites' ongoing invasion. They used the treaty proceedings to articulate their competing geographies and argue for their national sovereignty in the Tennessee Country.

Continuing their diplomatic strategy begun during past negotiations with British administrators, Cherokees believed that a formal border, enforced by the United States, was the only way to check the hordes of white intruders. "The white people have encroached on our lands, on every side of us," according to Chescoenwhee, who was there representing the Overhill town of Tomotly. He hoped that the United States would "adjust and settle our limits, so that we may be secured in the possession of our own . . . lands." Cherokees insisted that they alone possessed the authority to outline their nation's international borders. "We will mark a line for the white people," insisted Old Tassel and Tuskegatahee,

Nancy Ward's brother, who had only recently returned to the Overhills from the Chickamauga communities. During their week-long negotiation, Cherokees outlined a boundary line that arced from the confluence of the Duck and Tennessee Rivers northeast to the Kentucky Country and then back southeast toward the headwaters of the Oconee River in what would become northern Georgia. Parts of the border had been included in Cherokees' previous negotiations, but the Hopewell Treaty signified a consolidation of the entire boundary that would divide the United States from the Cherokee Nation. Old Tassel lectured American commissioners that they "must know the red people are the aborigines of this land," making it clear that Cherokees' right to their territory stemmed from their very indigeneity. Cherokee delegates considered national boundaries so important that Old Tassel drew a map for the U.S. commissioners. It was a forceful strategy to assert territorial control and would have been familiar to the American commissioners because of European powers' reliance on maps to project their imperial claims.[25]

The Chickasaw delegation similarly articulated their national boundaries in negotiations with the U.S. officials at Hopewell. Though some British Loyalists had fled into the Chickasaw Nation during the revolution, white Americans had only recently begun to intrude on their territory and in much smaller numbers than those faced by the Cherokees. Piominko did mention white encroachment, but access to U.S. trade goods was the Chickasaws' main priority at Hopewell. Clear borders were also important. When the U.S. commissioners produced Old Tassel's map of Cherokee boundaries, Piominko was unsatisfied because it did not demarcate the Chickasaws' entire international border. He "wished Congress would point out his lands to him; he wanted to know his own." Instead of allowing the Chickasaws to describe their national territory, the U.S. commissioners merely told the Chickasaw leaders that they "must agree with the neighboring tribes respecting their boundary," which could be determined at a later date.[26]

Negotiations at Hopewell may have ended with clear boundaries between the United States and Native southerners, but they set the stage for subsequent disagreements about where, and even if, the Cherokee-Chickasaw border existed. Although treaties with both nations outlined their boundaries with the United States, neither included a description of a border between the two Indigenous peoples. Even during negotiations, Cherokee commissioners Old Tassel and Tuskegatahee worried that Chickasaws were going to claim an exclusive right to territory in the Cumberland Valley around Nashville. They insisted that the region "is a kind of common right in all the Indians, and [the Chickasaws] had no right of

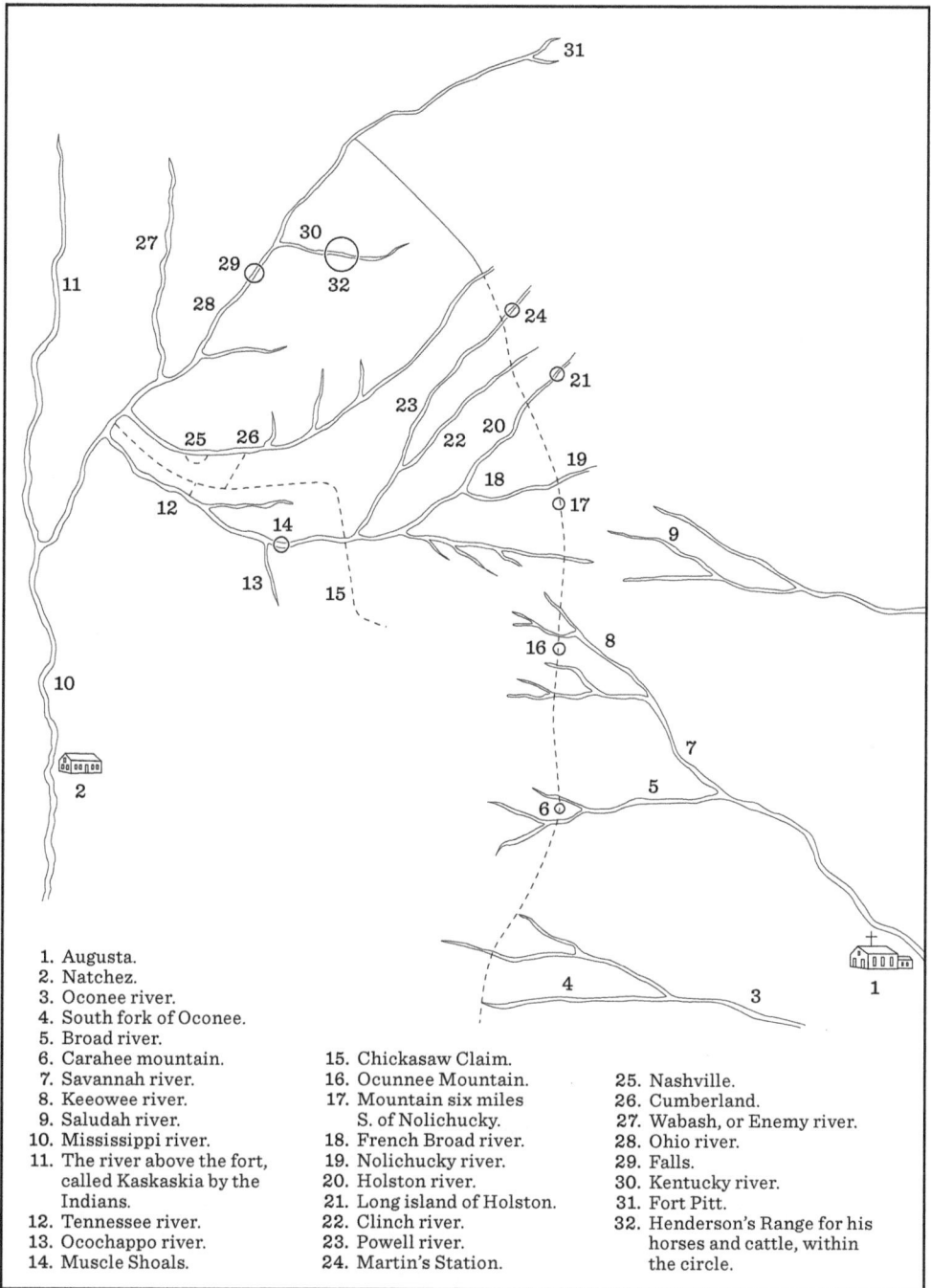

1. Augusta.
2. Natchez.
3. Oconee river.
4. South fork of Oconee.
5. Broad river.
6. Carahee mountain.
7. Savannah river.
8. Keeowee river.
9. Saludah river.
10. Mississippi river.
11. The river above the fort, called Kaskaskia by the Indians.
12. Tennessee river.
13. Ocochappo river.
14. Muscle Shoals.
15. Chickasaw Claim.
16. Ocunnee Mountain.
17. Mountain six miles S. of Nolichucky.
18. French Broad river.
19. Nolichucky river.
20. Holston river.
21. Long island of Holston.
22. Clinch river.
23. Powell river.
24. Martin's Station.
25. Nashville.
26. Cumberland.
27. Wabash, or Enemy river.
28. Ohio river.
29. Falls.
30. Kentucky river.
31. Fort Pitt.
32. Henderson's Range for his horses and cattle, within the circle.

The Cherokee Nation, adapted from the map created by Old Tassel in November 1785, which is published in the *American State Papers*. Old Tassel drew his map during the Hopewell negotiations. The dashed line on the map's right is the Cherokee-U.S. border. Chickasaws' "Claim" is shown by the dashed line labeled no. 15, though it is noticeably ambiguous. Map by Erin Greb Cartography on behalf of the author.

themselves" to allow Americans to live there. Before leaving the treaty ground, the Cherokees did define a "Chickasaw claim" on Old Tassel's map of the region and admitted that the Chickasaws were sovereign over land south of a line drawn from the Duck River's confluence with the Tennessee River to a point on a ridge dividing the Cumberland and Tennessee watersheds.[27] Chickasaws never agreed to this arbitrary and ill-defined boundary. The United States, however, had little incentive to survey an international border between Native nations because such a line would have no bearing on Americans' access to Indigenous land in the mid-1780s. This lack of spatial clarity foreshadowed a decades-long conflict between the two Native nations over their overlapping territories in the Tennessee Country.

The Counterrevolution against Federal Indian Policy

North Carolina speculators recognized the Hopewell Treaties' threat to their property claims across the Appalachian Mountains. Before negotiations began, Governor Caswell appointed William Blount as North Carolina's representative to attend the Hopewell conference. Blount was a good choice to defend speculators' interests. In addition to his Tennessee Company venture in the Great Bend, he and his brothers possessed claims to enormous amounts of Chickasaw territory acquired through North Carolina's land law of 1783. "I am sorry to find that the Chickasaws are coming to treaty," wrote Blount from Hopewell, "because [of] how much of North Carolina they claim and how disagreeable it will be to have a line fixed with them." Blount leveraged his personal connections with commissioner Joseph Martin in hopes that he would pressure Chickasaws to cede land along the Cumberland River, likely so that Blount's claims would not decrease in value. Indigenous sovereignty threatened Blount's personal finances, and he was quick to notify the U.S. Indian commissioners of North Carolinians' widespread opposition to a treaty that would recognize Native peoples' rights to any land within the state. Speculators like Blount rested their claims to the Tennessee Country on North Carolina's jurisdiction over territory from the Atlantic Ocean to the Mississippi River, guaranteed originally in the colony's charter and reinforced in its state constitution. The Articles of Confederation did not allow the federal commissioners to relinquish North Carolinians' landed property to Chickasaws or Cherokees. Before leaving Hopewell, Blount issued formal protests because the treaties prevented North Carolina speculators from accessing their property rights to Indigenous territory.[28]

At the behest of state legislators, North Carolina's congressional delegation subsequently convinced Congress to agree that the state's "territorial claims" remained valid. Hugh Williamson, one of North Carolina's representatives and himself a speculator in western land, celebrated that Congress's decision "leaves by implication every claim of the State in its usual force." North Carolina "only has to buy a further claim of soil from the Indians."[29] North Carolinians retained their property rights even as their land was inaccessible within the Cherokee and Chickasaw Nations, outside the jurisdiction of the United States. The Hopewell Treaties may have impeded speculators' commodification of the Tennessee Country. But Congress's decision to confirm the North Carolina grants within Chickasaw and Cherokee territory implied the inevitability of further expansion and undermined Indigenous nations' permanent sovereignty over their national lands.

The plight of local settlers was much more dire than that faced by distant speculators. The Cherokee Nation's treaty overturned Franklinites' coerced border created at the Treaty of Dumplin Creek six months before, leaving numerous white settlers within Cherokees' negotiated boundaries. Even Greeneville, Franklin's new capital, was on land now guaranteed to the Cherokee Nation by the federal government. Instead of accepting the new boundary and increased federal involvement in Native diplomacy, Franklin leaders doubled down on their pursuit of a settler empire. They responded to the Hopewell Treaties with violence and conquest. While the nation's leaders were away at the treaty ground, Franklin militia forces under Sevier's command raided nearby Cherokee towns. According to Old Tassel, Sevier promised to return later in the spring to "take our hunting Land from us and settell at the Mushel Shoales" in the Great Bend of the Tennessee River. Franklin leaders' state-building project aligned with the ongoing speculation of the Tennessee Company. For even as Sevier led the breakaway state government, he maintained correspondence with his eastern speculator allies, including Caswell, who had begun his second term as North Carolina governor in May 1785.[30]

Natives resisted settlers' ongoing colonization attempts. Chickamauga Cherokees and Creeks raided American settlements along the Cumberland River and in the southern reaches of the State of Franklin, retaliating for whites' recent encroachment and avenging the murder of four Cherokees earlier in 1786. The combined Creek and Chickamauga attacks were so successful that Tennessee Company officials had to delay another trip to the Great Bend because no one would "Venture to So dangerous a place." Instead of confronting the powerful Creek-Chickamauga alliance, Franklinites set their sights on the nearby Overhill Cherokees, despite their public assurances of peace. Franklin militia destroyed Cherokee communities along the Hiwassee River in the spring and summer of 1786.[31]

Meeting at Chota and Coyatee in late July and August, prominent Franklin officers threatened further raids if Overhill leaders would not accept the new borders coerced at the Treaty of Dumplin Creek a year earlier. William Cocke, Alexander Outlaw, Samuel Wear, and two other Franklinites referenced recent Chickamauga and Creek attacks as an excuse for violent retaliation against Overhill Towns. They lied that North Carolina had "sold us all the Country on the North Side of Tennessee and Holston" Rivers, despite the 1783 state law that established the reservation of Cherokee lands over much of these watersheds. Franklin negotiators appropriated the narrative of U.S. conquest to denounce Cherokee sovereignty. They repeated the standard refrain that victory over British forces allowed Americans to dictate peace terms to Britain's Native allies, but then they applied such notions of conquest to Franklin militia's recent destruction of Cherokee towns. "We have a right to all the ground we marched over" in a recent raid on peaceful Overhill Towns, proclaimed Franklin commissioners, because "taking of it by the Sword . . . is the best Right to all Countries." The white expansionists agreed to halt violent attacks only if Old Tassel and Hanging Maw (Scolacutta), an Overhill Cherokee leader of growing prominence from Coyatee, would agree to a boundary line with the State of Franklin that reached much lower down the Tennessee Valley than the U.S.-Cherokee border negotiated at Hopewell. Although the two Native leaders refused to accept blame for recent Cherokee attacks, they did sign the Treaty of Coyatee on August 3, 1786. Franklin leaders cheered their negotiations at Coyatee as a vindication of whites' property rights to stolen Native land.[32]

The Treaty of Coyatee only perpetuated the existing tension between local whites' expansionist demands and federal and state leaders' attempts to control Tennessee Valley settlers. Alexander Outlaw, a signatory of the agreement, refused to acknowledge congressional authority over the region. The Hopewell Treaty had improperly given land to the Cherokees; Franklinites had corrected the mistake with the Treaty of Coyatee. Outlaw believed that he and other Franklin negotiators could convince Cherokees to cede all of their land "to the georgia Line," which would "Shet the Eyes of Congress from [Lusting] after that Cuntry which I think is Our just righ[t]." Local whites' demand for the Tennessee Valley made irrelevant state and federal opposition to ongoing colonization. "Is not the Continent of America, one Day, to become one consolidated Government of United States?" David Campbell asked Governor Caswell. If so, then the United States had an obligation to extend its laws over white settlements in Native territory, including the five hundred settlers currently living on Cherokee land in clear violation of federal treaties and North Carolina law. "It is vain to say they must be restrained," concluded Campbell.[33]

Rather than restraint, Franklin leaders actively encouraged Americans' invasion of Native territory. In the wake of the Coyatee Treaty, the breakaway state created a local land office for territory south of the French Broad and Tennessee Rivers. To make it possible for cash-strapped settlers to acquire property, Franklin assemblymen allowed buyers to purchase land with animal furs and gave them two years to pay the full principal amount. Loyal North Carolina officials in the region worried about the potential for violence because white intruders now could lay claim to Cherokee cornfields and even portions "of their beloved Town Chota." By March 1787, Franklinites were already carving out new homesteads within the Cherokee Nation's northernmost territory.[34]

Franklin officials likely considered such expansionist land policies necessary to maintain popular support. Before 1787, white settlers streaming south over the French Broad and Tennessee Rivers had little hope of ever acquiring title to their settlements because the region was included in North Carolina's 1783 Cherokee reservation. Cherokees never accepted such a reduction of their nation's land, and North Carolina legislators did not issue any land grants within the reservation's bounds. Franklin's land office could, therefore, provide at least a veneer of legality to white encroachment and, in the process, guarantee settlers' loyalty to the expansionist state, given that their property rights to Native land depended entirely on the State of Franklin's survival. Intruders in the Cherokee Nation remained steadfast in their support for Franklin even after many local leaders reaffirmed their loyalty to North Carolina.[35] For these settler colonists, the expansionist geography included in the Treaty of Coyatee was a much better representation of their imperial wishes than the restrictive federal Indian policy included in the Hopewell Treaties.

———

Native peoples had their own interpretations of local whites' ongoing expansion and the role of American governance in that process. Though they had signed the Treaty of Coyatee, Old Tassel and Hanging Maw took no notice of the agreement's legitimacy nor that of the State of Franklin as a whole. Instead, Cherokees contacted North Carolina and U.S. officials to satisfy obligations included in their Hopewell Treaty. Only a month after the Coyatee meeting, Old Tassel and Hanging Maw pleaded with Governor Caswell to "Take your people of[f] our lands before they plant any more corn." Instead of respecting the Cherokees' border, whites "are comeing nearer [and] have settled close to our Towns." Caswell responded by issuing a proclamation in February ordering the removal of white intruders from the Cherokee Nation, which only served to further alienate Franklinites from North Carolina. As months passed with no border enforcement, Cherokees grew increasingly frustrated with Congress. "We have held Several treaties with the americans," protested Hanging Maw, "when Bounds was always fixt and fair promises always made that the white people should not come over, but we always find that after a treaty they Settle much faster than before." Cherokees demanded justice. If North Carolina or the United States continued to take no action against white intruders, then they might join Creeks and other Indigenous peoples in a war to regain their Tennessee Country territory.[36]

Chickasaws shared Cherokee displeasure with the United States. Piominko complained in early 1787 that the federal government had yet to fulfill its trading obligations with the Chickasaw Nation in accordance with their own Hopewell Treaty. The lack of goods left Chickasaws vulnerable to Creek attacks and made it increasingly likely that the Chickasaws, along with their Choctaw neighbors, would cultivate closer ties with Spain as a more reliable trading partner. "What can you expect us to do," asked Piominko, "as we have nothing but Letters passing and no ammonition to Defend ourselves with?" Piominko also understood that events in the Cherokee Nation could set a dangerous precedent for all of the Native South. "We are sorry to Heare that the White People are setling all the Lands Belonging to our Brothers the Cherokees," he explained. "We hope Something will be Done to Prevent it as we Expect when all their Lands is Settled our Lands will Go the Same way. . . . we are all Very Uneasy About it as we are told the Americans Intends to take All our Country Before they are Done." Piominko recognized the danger posed by Americans' settler empire. Their disregard for Native sovereignty and treaty agreements imperiled the diplomatic ties between his nation and the United States. Chickasaw leaders, including Taski Etoka and Tuskau Pautapau, who believed that the nation's interests would be better served through a stronger connection with Spain, were already demanding that Americans stop intruding on "our Hunting Grounds as it is our whole Dependance for . . . ourselves & families."[37] By 1787, then, Cherokees and Chickasaws wanted a more active federal government that could protect their property rights and enforce the orderly Hopewell Treaties against white inhabitants of the Tennessee Country.

Chapter 3

The Federal Government's Failings in the Tennessee Country

Philadelphia was not the only location for momentous deliberations in the summer of 1787. While American delegates to the Constitutional Convention debated a new governmental system to replace the Articles of Confederation, Chickasaw and Cherokee leaders were similarly thinking about their nations' futures. In late spring, a group of twenty Shawnee, Wyandot, and Mohawk ambassadors traveled south in hopes of adding Chickasaws and Choctaws to their Native confederacy and strengthening their existing ties with Creeks and Chickamaugas. Chickasaw leaders remained committed to peace. Cherokees, however, spent much more time considering the possibility of a military alliance. In a June conference, a Shawnee ambassador presented assembled Cherokee leaders with "a large belt of Wampam" as a symbol of their peoples' diplomatic ties. He hoped Cherokees would take part in an upcoming conference in the Creek Nation. These Native diplomats approached Indigenous unity strategically. They held the conference at Ustanali, a relatively new town established near the confluence of the Coosawattee and Conasauga Rivers. Not only was the community within an easy journey for Chickamauga Cherokees living along the Tennessee River fifty miles to the northwest, but the Cherokee inhabitants of Ustanali and other surrounding towns were also refugees from Georgia and South Carolina, who likely would be more receptive to talk of war against American invaders. Ustanali was eclipsing Chota as the most significant town in the nation, a transition that reflected the ongoing consolidation of Overhill, Middle, Out, and Valley communities into the Upper Town Cherokees caused by destructive militia campaigns and past land cessions. Northern Native diplomats thus spoke their message of unity in a town of national importance and to a Cherokee audience with firsthand experience of the destructive power of American expansion. Cherokees discussed the Native diplomats' proposal for eight days and even held an additional conference with Creeks, Mohawks, and Shawnees in the Creek Nation. Like the Chickasaws, they eventually decided to pursue peace with the Tennessee Country's white residents.[1]

Chickasaw and Cherokee officials believed a public rejection of violence might check Americans' ongoing invasion of their lands. Likely gathered at Long Town in the headwaters of the Tombigbee watershed, Chickasaws informed John Sevier, now governor of the State of Franklin, that they would not form alliances with Native peoples of the Ohio Valley. "Our desire is to live in peace with all white people and let the Red people that seeks war on themselves fight their own battles," explained Taski Etoka. Yet Chickasaws knew that white inhabitants of the Tennessee Country, including Sevier himself, coveted territory near the "Great Bend of the Tennessee." Tuskau Pautapau wanted Sevier to understand that Chickasaws remained on good terms with the Creek Nation, despite Creeks' ongoing attacks against American settlements. "We are your friends as well as theirs," explained Tuskau Pautapau, "therefore I am to desire you to keep your people from settling anywhere on our lands and hunting grounds." Chickasaws might join the Native alliance if Americans continued to violate their sovereignty. Cherokees announced a similar commitment to peace. Tuskegatahee, the former Chickamauga leader, explained that he presently wore an American medal around his neck as proof of his friendly intentions toward the United States. Nevertheless, Tuskegatahee warned Virginia's governor that he would fight—albeit reluctantly—should Americans continue to invade his nation without being punished. Cherokee and Chickasaw diplomats' maneuvers in the summer of 1787 proved that many believed their nations' survival depended on international alliances and possible military resistance against the United States should Americans continue to ignore their sovereign limits.[2]

News of the Cherokees' conference in the Creek Nation terrified settlers in the Tennessee Country. Nashville militia officers cried out for aid from Franklin, Georgia, Kentucky, and North Carolina. Farther east, Franklinites renewed plans to build a fort along the Hiwassee River and man it with soldiers paid with a land bounty of four hundred acres, presumably within Cherokee territory. Americans' ongoing invasion was the reason for the Chickamauga alliance with the Creeks, but Tennessee Valley whites felt that further encroachment could best protect their settlements from Native attacks.[3]